"Ever wonder about how God gui⸢
Then *God Told Me* is for you. In t
and carefully guides you through.
about God's guidance, using a myriad of exam⸗
you to rely more on him. And that is a very good thing."

Darrell Bock, research professor of New Testament studies,
Dallas Theological Seminary

"Listening is more than an art . . . it is a necessity. Just ask my wife, who often wonders if I have lost my hearing. Part of mastering the necessity of listening is to recognize the important voices in your life and train your heart to listen intently to them. For those of us who are followers of Christ, listening to his voice and the voice of God our father is critically important to a flourishing relationship with him. My friend Jim Samra has unraveled the often tangled mystery of recognizing God's voice and learning to follow it, to the joy of a deeper, more rewarding life as we walk according to the beat of his voice."

Dr. Joseph M. Stowell, president, Cornerstone University,
Grand Rapids, Michigan

"Evangelicals are comfortable talking about their personal relationship with God, but decidedly uneasy when it comes to saying 'God told me so.' Jim Samra boldly contends that God speaks to people today to provide concrete guidance, and he is careful to root his argument in Scripture rather than personal experience, though the latter, his own and others', provides plenty of colorful illustrations. *God Told Me* is an important contribution to debates about decision making and the will of God, a practical guide to the process of seeking divine guidance, and, more importantly, a testimony to the extraordinary shape of the ordinary Christian life."

Kevin J. Vanhoozer, Blanchard Professor of Theology,
Wheaton College Graduate School

"If you desire to hear and recognize the voice of God in the flow of your daily life, you will love this book. If you believe God speaks, but are not sure how to be confident you are receiving heavenly direction, this book will bring clarity to your listening process. If you hunger for a life guided by God, this book will fill you with biblical and practical food for thought. *God Told Me* is a valuable tool for anyone who wants to hear and follow the voice of God."

Kevin G. Harney, pastor of Shoreline Community Church
and author of *Reckless Faith*

God told me

who to marry,
where to work,
which car to buy . . .
and I'm pretty sure
I'm not *crazy*

JIM SAMRA

BakerBooks

a division of Baker Publishing Group
Grand Rapids, Michigan

© 2012 by Jim Samra

Published by Baker Books
a division of Baker Publishing Group
P.O. Box 6287, Grand Rapids, MI 49516-6287
www.bakerbooks.com

Printed in the United States of America

Library of Congress Cataloging-in-Publication Data
Samra, James George, 1972–
    God told me : who to marry, where to work, which car to buy . . . and I'm
pretty sure I'm not crazy / Jim Samra.
      p. cm.
    Includes bibliographical references (p.   ).
    ISBN 978-0-8010-1411-6 (pbk.)
      1. Discernment (Christian theology) 2. God (Christianity)—Will.
    3. Listening—Religious aspects—Christianity. I. Title.
    BV4509.5.S253 2012
    248.4—dc23   2012005943

12   13   14   15   16   17   18   7   6   5   4   3   2   1

To Lisa

contents

acknowledgments

This is a book that has been fashioned and formed over many years, and there are many people for whom I am grateful.

First, there are the Christians throughout history who willingly listened to God and told their stories. Sometimes I've thought I was crazy, but when I read about George Müller, Charles Spurgeon, Hudson Taylor, Francis of Assisi, Polycarp, or Darlene Rose, I am reminded that it is crazy to think God *wouldn't* speak words of guidance to his children.

Likewise, I am grateful to all the people who allowed their stories to be shared in this book. It is impossible to learn to recognize God's voice without having examples to learn from. Thank you for being willing to share what God told you. In the same way, I am thankful for Calvary Church, a gathering of brothers and sisters in Christ where I have been able to listen to God's voice and share that with the congregation. Calvary is also a church where God is regularly speaking to others—and they are listening. What a great church!

I am grateful to my parents, who listened intently for God's leading in raising me and in doing so taught me to expect God to answer. My father, especially, set the example with this. What a blessing to grow up in a family led by a man who sought God's guidance for the decisions of life!

Thank you to the people at Baker Books. You will not be surprised to know that God told me to publish this book with them. God used a noon lunch with Jack Kuhatschek to guide me into working with Baker, with Jack as editor, to publish this book. The choice of Jack was not accidental. He, like me, had attended Dallas Theological Seminary, where a different model of making decisions was in vogue, despite the fact that the school was founded through men of God listening for God's guidance as presented here. Jack was a wonderful discussion partner who sharpened much of what is written here. So, too, I am thankful for others at Baker, including Ruth Anderson and Mike Cook, who sought God's guidance with regard to marketing this book. Thanks to Lindsey Spoolstra and others who carefully read through the book making valuable editing suggestions.

Others have read the book and provided great encouragement and help, including the pastoral staff at Calvary, Kevin VanHoozer, Kent Snoeyink, Mike Dokter, the guys at SAET, and others. This book wouldn't be nearly what it is without them.

To my four children: George, Grace, Abigail, and James. Thank you for all the joy and love you bring to our family. Your mother and I are working diligently to hear God's voice for you, but our prayer is that you will grow up to recognize God's voice for yourselves and learn to love him as your Good Shepherd.

And what can I say about my amazing wife, to whom this book is dedicated? The story of God arranging our marriage is a beautiful testament to God's guiding power, but it is also a testament to Lisa's willingness to trust God's guidance and direction—willingness that she has continued to display for our children to see. Seeking God's leading has been the much more difficult road: the waiting, the uncertainty, the faith-stretching paths God has taken us down, and the strange looks and comments from others who don't understand. Through it all she has been a model of godliness. I am only beginning to recognize the wisdom of God in selecting her for me. Even if there were no other examples of God's guidance in my life, this one alone would be sufficient for me to believe our God is a guiding God.

Most of all, I am thankful to God. He has been my Guide every step of the way. He has taught me to hear his voice. Faithfully, time and again, he has spoken into my darkness and confusion and brought the light of clear direction. I look back at where he has taken me and I am awed by his incredible wisdom and love. The reason I have written this book, and my earnest prayer, is for every Christian to know the joy of hearing the voice of the Good Shepherd leading them to still waters.

introduction

God told me to write this book.

And I'm pretty sure I'm not crazy.

People regularly claim that God communicates specific guidance to them. In our church alone, I think of Joan, who claims God told her that her husband was going to live, despite the life-threatening situation he was facing. Chad and Paula believe God told them to buy the house they now live in. Kay believes God told her he had just taken her beloved, elderly mother to be with him, reassuring and comforting her before the phone call came. Toran and Brenda think God told them to adopt a special needs child named Max. The worship planning committee one Sunday felt God specifically told them to sing the song "Great Is Thy Faithfulness" during one of the worship services, which spoke words of comfort to a young father struggling with a child teetering on the brink of death. Bruce believes that, within days of his meeting her, God revealed to him he would marry Debbie, who has now been his wife for thirty-four years.

These claims are not limited to our church, or even to our period of history. In the second century Polycarp believed that God told him he was going to die a martyr's death.[1] In the fourth century Augustine recorded that God told him to pick up the Bible and read the first section he opened to, Romans 13:13–14, which caused him to come to faith.[2] In the thirteenth century Edmund of Abingdon switched from studying math to theology on the basis of a dream from God.[3] In the nineteenth century Hudson Taylor claimed that God told him to be a missionary to China. Holman Hunt stated that God guided him in his painting.[4] Charles Spurgeon maintained that God tells people with whom to share the gospel and gave him the texts on which he was supposed to preach.[5] George Müller often stated that God told him to start orphanages.[6] In the early half of the twentieth century Francis Schaeffer believed God told him to go to college and train to be a minister despite his father's ardent opposition.[7] Lewis Sperry Chafer testified that God told him to start Dallas Theological Seminary.[8]

These examples could be multiplied a thousand times over, and not just from my life, our church, this century, or the history of the church. The Bible relates hundreds of examples of such things: God told Joshua that Achan's sin was the reason Israel was unsuccessful in their battle at Ai (see Josh. 7). God not only told Israel that Saul was to be their first king, but also that he was hiding among the baggage (see 1 Sam. 10:22). God told Daniel how long Israel was going to be in captivity and what was to happen after that period of exile (see Dan. 9). God the Father told Jesus which disciples to choose as apostles (see John 17:6–12; Luke 6:12–15). God told Philip to go to the chariot of the Ethiopian eunuch and stay near it (see Acts 8:29). God told Paul to stay out of Bithynia and work in Macedonia (see Acts 16).

What are we to make of these claims that "God told me"? We have no problem recognizing that God spoke to people in the Bible, and we might be willing to concede that God has spoken at unique times in church history, but what about today? Does God speak to people today about such things? How can someone listen to God's guidance? How do we know when we have heard from God?

God Speaks

Clearly God has spoken in the past, and he did so for a variety of reasons. God spoke to create life (see Gen. 1), he spoke to make covenants (see Gen. 12:1–3), he spoke to communicate his moral demands (see Exod. 19), he spoke to rebuke and encourage his people (see Jer. 1:1–9), and he spoke to communicate the future (see Matt. 24).

And clearly God continues to speak today. God speaks through creation to declare his glory (see Ps. 19:1–4). The Holy Spirit speaks to the world, convicting men and women of sin, righteousness, and judgment (see John 16:8). The Holy Spirit speaks to Christians, testifying that we are children of God (see Rom. 8:16). God speaks through his Word (and by the Holy Spirit) to teach, rebuke, correct, and train (see 2 Tim. 3:16) as well as to convict and judge (see Heb. 4:12).

But there is one particular purpose for which God spoke in the past and, I believe, still speaks today that is far too often neglected: to provide guidance. Not guidance as to what is right and wrong (he does that too), but guidance for the decisions of life such as where to live, whom to marry, what job to take, the best way to endure suffering, with whom to share the gospel, and the like. This is an aspect of God speaking.

Warning!

At this point, for some, warning bells may be going off in your heads. The idea of God's guidance conjures up an image of a seemingly pious person sitting in their car at a stop sign fervently fasting and praying, asking God to please tell them whether they should turn right or left in order to get to work, immobilized by their refusal to choose until they have received a word from the Lord.

Let me say up front that there are thousands of decisions all of us make on a daily basis for which the guidance of God is subtle and unnoticed. A neighbor's child knocks on our door selling wrapping paper for a school fundraiser. Hoping to be a good witness for Christ and a good neighbor, we decide then and there to purchase the wrapping paper. God has allowed us as Christians to have the mind of Christ, and in that moment we make a Christ-honoring decision without even stopping to think about it. Likewise, God has given us the ability to learn our driving route to work. When we pull up to a stop sign we immediately access our God-given wisdom and turn right without out a moment's hesitation.

The Bible is filled with examples of this sort of implicit decision-making process. For example, when Paul arrived in Thessalonica he didn't stop at the city gate and ask God, "What am I supposed to do?" Instead, he went into the synagogue and started preaching the gospel, "as was his custom" (Acts 17:2). This is not to say that God didn't lead him to preach in the synagogue. God's leading and guiding were seamless and unconscious, coming through Paul's intimate relationship with the Spirit dwelling within him.

However, there are many examples in the biblical narrative and the witness of history where the process of God's guidance in non-moral decisions is much more deliberate, noticeable, and conscious, with God either initiating the communication or responding to a request for guidance. In Acts 16, God spoke to Paul in a vision, directly guiding him to go to Macedonia and preach the gospel. Paul didn't just go "as was his custom," but because God took the initiative and told him in a more tangible and conscious process to go to Macedonia. Likewise, earlier in Acts the eleven apostles needed help in selecting a replacement for Judas Iscariot. Bathing their decision in prayer, the apostles took the initiative and asked God to select for them the twelfth apostle (see Acts 1:24–26). This process of seeking God's guidance was deliberate, intentional, and explicit.

It is these more explicit and deliberate times of being guided by God that I am focusing on in this book. While the vast majority of decisions made in the Bible and throughout history are those where God's Spirit works subtly with our spirit to lead us in ways that we may not even be aware of, there are a significant number of times when God's guidance is much more explicit and the process of choosing much more deliberate. Examples of these include situations such as when Hudson Taylor wanted to know where to be a missionary, when Rebekah wanted counsel on why she was having such trouble with her pregnancy (see Gen. 25:22–23), or when we want to know what house to buy.

The differentiating feature, however, is not the magnitude of the decisions. After all, the eternal consequences of Paul choosing to go into the synagogue at Thessalonica were just as great as him choosing Macedonia over Bithynia. Rather, the differentiating feature is our need or desire for specific, explicit guidance from God. We might long for (or God might determine we need) more explicit guidance for a variety of reasons. Perhaps God wants us to follow an unusual path. Perhaps we need more tangible assurance of God's leading. Perhaps we are more conscious of our inability to know what to do in a particular area.

Whatever the reason, there are times when we need more explicit guidance from God, and in such situations we need to know: Why should we go to God for guidance and how do we do it? How do we recognize when God is responding? How can we inquire of God and be able to say with confidence "God led me"?

My Personal Story

Listening for explicit guidance from God for certain decisions has been a process for me over a twenty-year period, and as we begin, I want to give you a sense of the period of my life during which these ideas first began to germinate.

The first time I was conscious of hearing God's guiding voice, I was eighteen years old and, like many, clueless as to what I should do with my life. Although I became a Christian at a young age, and God was present in my life behind the scenes, guiding many of the decisions I made, it never crossed my mind to ask God what he thought I should do with my life. Wasn't

God only interested in whether or not I obeyed his rules? When I prayed it was to ask him to help me not be such a coward in sharing the gospel or to help me get through stressful situations. It never dawned on me that God might actually be interested in guiding the path of my life.

But at eighteen, having just shared a testimony in my church about God's faithfulness for graduation Sunday, I found myself being asked by a complete stranger what I was going to be studying in college. Embarrassed because I had no answer and sure I would never see him again, I did the only rational thing. I lied. My older brother was an engineer and always got positive feedback when he told adults that, so I told the man I was going to be an engineer, even though it was the one thing I had vowed never to do (the academics scared me to death, as did the social life).

A few months later, I went to my orientation session at the University of Michigan. When I arrived, I was in a group with all engineering students and an engineering advisor, even though I most certainly was not in the college of engineering. This advisor urged me to sign up for basic math and science classes, reasoning that they would transfer to any degree, including engineering. At this point I began to wonder if God was trying to tell me something.

Midway through my freshman year, while still enrolled in my liberal arts program, that complete stranger to whom I had lied about being an engineering major sought out my parents at church one Sunday. He oversaw the engineering internships at Steelcase and wondered if I wanted to apply for one. Faced with the alternative of returning to my local grocery store and again working the dreaded bottle return counter for minimum wage, I applied for the engineering internship, praying for God to show me if this was from him. And miraculously, I was hired.

Knowing that this was not coming from me, I began to sense God was guiding me to transfer to the engineering school and major in mechanical engineering. This was my first experience with consciously recognizing God's leading.

My fear of the academics associated with engineering was not without cause. Not surprisingly, I soon found myself in way over my head. Failing was a very real option—and I was petrified of failure. So, as only an eighteen-year-old could, I made a deal with God. If I didn't study enough and flunked out, I would take the blame. If I studied a reasonable amount of time, but still failed, I was going to blame God. If, however, I studied enough and God got me through, I would give him all the glory for it. And, when I graduated, I would use my engineering degree in whatever way he wanted.

Four years went by and graduation loomed. It was clear God had held up his end of the deal. I was not only making it through the program, but actually thriving and loving it. Now I needed to fulfill my promise. But how was I supposed to find out what God wanted me to do with this engineering degree? God had gently pushed me into engineering by opening doors and arranging circumstances, so I decided to pursue four different options at once, confident that God would close all the doors but the one he wanted.

It didn't happen. All four doors opened. Now what? For months I had been praying generally, now I began to pray specifically, "Lord, which of these do you want me to choose?" No answer. I was confused and frustrated. Maybe God wasn't going to answer. I was tempted to just use human wisdom, make what I thought was the best decision, and call it good, even though this wasn't exactly what I had promised God. It was at this point I made one of life's fateful decisions.

Rattling around in my mind were the stories of the patriarch Jacob, who wrestled with God and refused to let him go until he blessed him, and the missionary Hudson Taylor, whose biography had impacted me deeply. In Jacob's case, I could identify with a "deceiver" whom God still guided and directed. In Hudson Taylor's case, I saw a man completely reliant on God for direct guidance in the decisions of his life. I wanted to live that way too, so I made my fateful decision. There would be no "Plan B" if God didn't answer my requests for guidance. I was not letting God go until he guided me, even if all four opportunities passed me by.

By then it was March. I was facing deadlines for the different opportunities and I needed to decide by March 16. As of March 12, I had not heard a peep from God. I was scared, but resolved.

On March 13, the phone rang. It was Texas Instruments inviting me for an interview. I tried to tell them no, but something in me said yes. I found myself on a plane to Dallas. Over the next two days in Dallas, God suddenly began to speak. The darkness melted away and I became completely convinced that God was telling me to move to Texas, begin working at Texas Instruments, and attend Dallas Theological Seminary. At this point, I was beginning to realize that while God was always faithful, listening for his guidance was not always straightforward or for the faint-of-heart. Little did I know that this was all just preparation for what was next.

Up until this point I had been essentially a bystander watching the whole boy-girl dating process. Reflecting on my very limited experience, and especially the experiences of others, I had become completely disillusioned with dating as a means of selecting a wife. During this time in Texas, I came across two Scriptures that would change my life forever. The first was in Genesis 24, where Isaac marries Rebekah, a bride whom God specifically chose for him. I remember thinking to myself, "Why couldn't God do that for me?" Of course, he *could*, but I wasn't sure if he would. After all, weren't Isaac and Rebekah part of a unique Bible story not to be repeated today? Being of Arab descent, the idea of an arranged marriage was not completely foreign. On occasions in the past my parents had half-jokingly offered to select a wife for me. As intriguing as an arranged marriage sounded at times, on the whole I was rather leery of entrusting this decision to my parents. But then I came across the passage in Matthew 7, where God says:

> Which of you, if your son asks for bread, will give him a stone? Or if he asks for a fish, will give him a snake? If you, then, though

you are evil, know how to give good gifts to your children, how much more will your Father in heaven give good gifts to those who ask him! (vv. 9–11)

Suddenly those words came alive to me. If my earthly father was even remotely interested in helping me find a spouse, then surely my heavenly Father would guide me if I asked him to. If the story of Isaac and Rebekah told me that God *could* choose a spouse for me, Matthew 7 encouraged me that he *would* if I asked. Inspired by this word from the Lord, I decided to ask God to arrange a marriage for me. My only request was that he choose someone I didn't know and tell me whom he had chosen before I saw her, because I didn't want my desires getting in the way of genuinely hearing from God.

Amazingly, he did just that. At the age of twenty-three, I found myself sitting in a graduate class listening to a professor offer a prayer request regarding his daughter, whom I had never met before and knew nothing about—I didn't even know her first name. Yet at that moment God gave me the strangest, most indescribably subjective impression that this mystery person was his choice for my spouse! I could not have been more surprised. Surely, this was some crazy notion I had dreamed up. But how could it be? I hadn't even known this professor had a daughter.

This impression stayed with me. Every time I thought I had dismissed the notion as irrational craziness, it would come back. Six months later I actually met her, first on the phone and only later in person. (I never mentioned anything to her about God arranging marriages though!) Over the next ten months God graciously confirmed his guidance in a number of remarkable and clear ways. By the time we got engaged, I was 100 percent positive God had chosen Lisa to be my wife. A year later we were married.

From that point on, Lisa and I have experienced God's guidance and direction in a myriad of different ways. God called us into ministry; guided us to a specific church for training; told us to sell our possessions and move overseas; selected a school and a supervisor for me; directly gave me a PhD topic; told us to stay in England and trust him when our son developed health problems; told us to move somewhere we never expected to live; told me to take a job I was horribly ill-prepared for; selected sermon series for me; guided me in staffing decisions; chose a house for us; led us on various trips and adventures; gave us guidance on how many children to have; and provided counsel and advice about ministry decisions, finances, schooling for our children, and so much more. Each one of these examples has its own story, some of which I'll talk about more later.

As I look back on this small sample of the times God has guided me, there is radiant joy in my heart. Although they are just words on the page to you, for me each story represents a personal encounter with the living God. Yet the darkness is greatest right before the dawn, and honestly, many of these experiences were incredibly hard. They represent periods of darkness and confusion, tearful agonizing and pleading with God for guidance, even enduring ridicule from other Christians who thought listening for guidance from God was misguided. Some represent debilitating fear as the realization of what God was saying dawned on me. Some recall long periods of waiting. Like the psalmist I often felt, "When my heart was grieved and my spirit embittered, I was senseless and ignorant; I was a brute beast before you" (Ps. 73:21–22). But each one of these stories also represents a dawning moment when the light of God's guidance shone. Incredibly, the living God spoke personally to me in my specific situation! He showed me where to go and gave me glimpses of what he was doing. And so with the psalmist, I can also proclaim, "Yet I am always with you; you hold me by my right hand. You guide me with your counsel, and afterward you will take me into glory. . . . My flesh and my heart may fail, but God is the strength of my heart and my portion forever" (Ps. 73:23–24, 26). There is almost no greater joy than to be in darkness and to hear God speak words of light, to be confused and to hear his voice of clarity. Peace is the best way to describe it.

Yet far too many Christians miss out on this. Some Christians are being led by the Spirit only in subconscious ways. To be led at all is wonderful, but sadly they have missed the overwhelming joy of actually hearing God speak to them, providing specific, explicit guidance. The problem is that we are in many ways children of the Enlightenment. Many of us are deists in practice, if not in theology.[9] We act as if God created the universe, handed us the instruction manual, and now doesn't want to be bothered with us again, as if he is some sort of absentee father. We do our thing; he does his. As long as we obey, he's happy. He's even willing to bail us out of a few fixes we might find ourselves in along the way.

But the Bible presents a far different picture: a warm, loving Father who is intimately interested in all aspects of our lives, actively making himself available to counsel and to guide. I want to share him with you.

The experiences and truths offered here are those of a fellow traveler. Even after twenty years of exploring God's guidance, I have not finished understanding it. While I learned in my arranged marriage that God can be trusted in the big decisions of life, I am still learning how to actively listen in smaller decisions. I am trying to become better at being open to his guiding at all times, even when I am not actively seeking it. No matter how many hundreds of times he has spoken specific guidance, I am still trying to learn not to be afraid that this time he won't. Most of all, I am still experiencing new ways in which God communicates his guidance to us. But I have learned enough from God's Word, my own experiences, and the experiences of others to share with you some things that will help you either start on this path or encourage you along the way.

The Plan

I have revealed a little of my own journey in hearing God speak, as well as hinted at the experiences of others. But I have not yet explained what exactly we mean when we say, "God guides," nor have I shared how we knew it was God and not our own voices, society, parents, or something else.

This book is broken up into two halves. The first half of the book explores the notion of receiving guidance from God by answering four big questions: What is guidance from God? (chapter 1), why should we seek guidance from God? (chapter 2), how does God provide guidance? (chapter 3), and how do we know when it is God who is speaking? (chapter 4).

In the second half of the book, I'll shift focus to explaining the process of listening for guidance from God. We'll talk about what we need to do to prepare to hear from the Lord (chapter 5), pointers on how to actively listen to God (chapter 6), lessons learned about the process of listening for guidance from God (chapter 7), and the issue of telling the stories of God's guidance to others (chapter 8). Then we'll finish with an appendix of some frequently asked questions.

Before we begin, let me make a comment about the stories in this book. I have included many stories throughout the book because there is no way to explain how God guides without illustrating it. That is why so much of what we learn about seeking guidance from God comes from the narrative sections of Scripture. I have also taught this material on many occasions, and people have commented that it is the stories that make all the difference.

These stories fall into four major groups. First, there are a large number of biblical stories. A majority of these stories come from the Old Testament simply because there is so much more narrative material in the Old Testament. Yet no one should infer that God's guidance is something confined to the Old Testament, because the highest percentage of examples comes from the book of Acts. (Examples of such guidance can also be found in the Gospels, as well as the narrative portions of epistles such as Galatians and 2 Corinthians). Second, there are many stories from missionaries, pastors, and Christian leaders in the church both today and throughout history. This is not because God guides only those who are in "full-time ministry."

Rather, it is simply because we don't have a lot of Christian businessperson biographies from the seventh century! Third, I have included many stories of everyday people with whom I am familiar. These stories come from people of all ages, in all walks of life, and with varying degrees of spiritual maturity and experience at hearing God's voice. Fourth, I have included a number of my own stories. This is not because I have done a better job of seeking God's guidance than others. Rather, I am most intimately familiar with my own stories. Part of the value of sharing stories is the ability to share the struggles and confusion of the process of hearing God's voice. For others' stories, I am often not privy to the details of the process of the decision, whereas with my own examples, I am.

The discovery of the truth that God graciously provides guidance and counsel for our lives has been among the most significant things to ever happen to me. I am excited to share that with you.

the four big questions

1

what is guidance from God?

t was 2002. I held a degree in engineering, of all things, from the University of Michigan. But here I was, sitting on the stage in the "overflow" seating of a packed lecture hall at Calvin College. I was in the midst of trying to decide where to go for graduate school—not for engineering, but for a PhD in theology. In God's providence I ended up a few yards from the speaker, renowned British New Testament scholar N. T. (Tom) Wright. My wife had squeezed into a seat in the balcony, but somehow I was on stage. As the lecture ended I spied an opportunity to ask the professor a few questions. As his handlers were hurrying him off the platform, I rushed forward, and began walking alongside him. As we walked, I said, "Can I ask your advice on something?"

"Sure," he responded.

"I have been accepted at different British schools to do PhD studies. Where would you recommend that I go?"

He asked a few questions about who my advisors would be at the various schools and what I would be studying. He listened to my responses, and then said, "This is a big decision and I don't know what other factors might be involved, but from what you have told me, if I were you I would go to Cambridge."

That's advice. Tom Wright was using the wisdom that he had accrued to provide me counsel. He did not say to me, "I am sure that whatever you choose will be just fine." That may have been true, but I had directly asked him for advice, not affirmation about my own decision-making ability. Neither did he say to me, "Where you go to school is not important, just make sure that when you get where you are going that you do not plagiarize." Such moral admonitions, while useful, have nothing to do with choosing a school. Nor did Dr. Wright simply brush me off. I was a confused student looking for help. He was older, wiser, more experienced, and a professor who had a far greater working knowledge of the British educational system than me. The gracious and kind thing for him to do was to give me a direct answer to a direct question, which he did.

But what if I had gone instead to God to ask for advice and counsel about which school I should attend? What should I have expected as a response from God? Should I have expected God to respond by reassuring me that whatever decision I made would be fine? Should I have expected him to tell me that where I went to school was not important; what mattered was that I not plagiarize when I got there? Should I have expected that God would have brushed me off and completely ignored my request? Or should I have expected a direct answer to a direct question, like the one I received from Tom Wright?

I did ask God, of course. But more on that later.

Like That of One Who Inquires of God

"Now in those days the advice Ahithophel gave was like that of one who inquires of God. That was how both David and Absalom regarded all of Ahithophel's advice" (2 Sam. 16:23).

In this passage about a little-known character from the time of King David, we find an important key to clarifying what it means to receive counsel from God. While the verse highlights the great value of Ahithophel's advice, an important inference from the verse is that advice we get from God is like the advice we get from others. If David wanted to know whether or not he should attack the Philistines, this verse implies he could have expected both Ahithophel and God to answer in the same way, with either a "yes," "no," or "not yet." This is the key idea for understanding the guidance that comes from God; we should expect to get the same kind of advice from God we expect to receive from other people, or give out ourselves.

When I say that advice from God is like the advice we receive from others, I don't mean the advice is of the same *quality*. I mean that it is of the same *kind*. In other words, if I ask my friend who is a real estate agent whether I should purchase a certain house at the price offered, the advice I would get from him, either, "Yes, this is a good deal," or "No, don't buy it at this price," is the same kind of advice I should expect from God, who may even choose to communicate his guidance through my friend (we will talk about this more in chapter 3). There are unique aspects to the advice we receive from God—namely, it will reflect his Lordship and infinite wisdom—but my point here is that we would still recognize it as guidance.

Not sure about this yet? Look with me at some examples from the Bible where God provided guidance and counsel.

Direct Guidance

In the book of Genesis, Abraham's chief servant was tasked by his master with finding a wife for Isaac. Abraham promised the servant that God's angel would guide him. Overwhelmed by the magnitude of his assignment, yet trusting in the words of Abraham, the servant turns to God and makes a direct request for guidance:

> See, I am standing beside this spring, and the daughters of the townspeople are coming out to draw water. May it be that when I say to a young woman, "Please let down your jar that I may

have a drink," and she says, "Drink, and I'll water your camels too"—let her be the one you have chosen for your servant Isaac. By this I will know that you have shown kindness to my master. (Gen. 24:13–14)

Before the servant can even finish praying, God answers. Rebekah appears and exactly fulfills the servant's request of the Lord. Here is a direct request for guidance and it is answered in the way we would expect—directly.

Rebekah herself, just one chapter (and twenty years) later, finds herself needing counsel from the Lord because her twin babies are constantly jostling in her womb. Confused, Rebekah goes to "inquire of the Lord." "Why is this happening to me?" she asks (Gen. 25:22). To this direct question God responds with a direct answer, telling her it is because "two nations are in your womb," and they will struggle against each other (v. 23).

Fast-forward hundreds of years. God has rescued Israel from bondage in Egypt, raising up Moses and leading him each step of the way. As God is leading the Israelites around the wilderness, Moses encounters a confusing case in his role as judge. A man named Zelophehad died in the wilderness, leaving four daughters and no sons. The daughters come to Moses and the elders, asking to inherit their father's property. No one knows what to do, so Moses brings the case before the Lord. God responds, "What Zelophehad's daughters are saying is right. They should inherit the land" (see Num. 27:1–11). A direct answer to a direct question.

More time passes, and we come to the era where Joshua is the leader of the Israelites and the nation is preparing to enter the land God promised to them. Their initial military battle against Jericho is a great success. Excitement is at a fever pitch as the Israelites anticipate their next victory. The next city, Ai, is so weak that Joshua is advised to send only a few thousand men. But shockingly Ai routs the Israelites (see Josh. 7). Joshua is utterly confused and horribly discouraged. He cries out to the Lord, "What are we supposed to do now?" This is the same kind of question that Joshua might have put to Moses if Moses had still been alive. Yet he can't ask Moses; instead he asks God. And God answers him directly, not only telling him that their defeat is a result of sin, but he identifies the specific person who had sinned, Achan. Again, God provides very specific guidance to lead Joshua to what he cannot know on his own.

Jump now to the time of Samuel and Saul (see 1 Sam. 9). Saul and his servant are out looking for some donkeys that have been lost. They have traveled all over and cannot find them. As they are getting ready to go home, Saul's servant suggests that they go to visit Samuel for divine guidance to help them find their donkeys. So off they go. Meanwhile, God has specifically told Samuel, "About this time tomorrow I will send you a man from the tribe of Benjamin. Anoint him leader over my people Israel." Samuel does so, following God's specific guidance.

(And, by the way, God also specifically answers Saul's request for information about his donkeys.)

Skip ahead again to the time of David. David seems to be constantly asking God for guidance. One series of examples can be found in 1 Samuel 23, when David asks the Lord, "Shall I go and attack these Philistines?" To which God replies, "Go, attack the Philistines and save Keilah" (v. 2). When David communicates God's guidance to his men, they think he has lost his mind. So David goes back to God to ask him the same question. Far from being angry, God reassures David that he will be victorious. And he is. But in Keilah, David begins to hear rumors that Saul is coming to trap him. Are these rumors true? Unsure of what to do, David begs God for counsel: "Will the citizens of Keilah surrender me to him? Will Saul come down, as your servant has heard? LORD, God of Israel, tell your servant" (v. 11). These are direct questions and David wants direct answers. He gets them: "And the LORD said, 'He will.' Again David asked, 'Will the citizens of Keilah surrender me and my men to Saul?' And the LORD said, 'They will'" (v. 11–12).

Jump ahead a few centuries to the time of Nehemiah. In grief over the ruined state of Jerusalem, Nehemiah is assigned to lead the rebuilding project. How should he go about doing it? Nehemiah tells us that God was guiding him, putting plans in his heart (see Neh. 2:12). When the work was completed Nehemiah faced another problem. There were not enough people living in Jerusalem. What should he do? "So my God gave me the idea of gathering the nobles, the officials, and the people to be registered by families" (see Neh. 7:5).[1] When Nehemiah needed specific, tangible plans for specific, tangible problems, God provided them.

Consider an example from the life of Jesus. In Luke 6:12 we are told that Jesus went off to a mountaintop to spend the night praying to God. Although we are not told explicitly what Jesus and the Father spoke about, the very next verse says, "When morning came, he called his disciples to him and chose twelve of them, whom he also designated as apostles" (v. 13). I. H. Marshall comments, "Thus the choice of the Twelve is made only after seeking God's guidance."[2] That's why Jesus says the Father is the one who ultimately chose the Twelve for him (see John 17:6). Jesus asked the Father who his apostles should be and God gave Jesus these twelve specific men.

Once we get to the book of Acts, the examples of specific guidance from God come cascading one on top of another. Consider a few.

In the case of Philip (see Acts 8:26–40), God tells him through an angel, "Go south to the road—the desert road—that goes down from Jerusalem to Gaza." Philip follows God's specific guidance. There he finds an Ethiopian riding a chariot and studying Isaiah. "Go up to the chariot and stay near it," the Spirit tells him. Recognizing that God has led him to this opportunity to share the gospel, Philip does so. Immediately afterward, the Spirit takes him to Azotus, to do further mission work starting from there.

Two chapters later, an angel of the Lord appears to Cornelius—a man who is not even a Christian—and tells him to send men to Joppa, to the home of Simon the Tanner whose house is by the sea, to bring back a man named Peter (see Acts 10:5–6).

The men show up at the exact time God has finished speaking to Peter in a dream. At the end of the dream the Spirit says to Peter, "Three men are looking for you. So get up and go downstairs. Do not hesitate to go with them for I have sent them" (vv. 19–20). Guidance can't get much more specific than that.

Finally, consider Paul when he is in the city of Ephesus, trying to decide where to go next (see Acts 19). The Bible tells us that he engaged in a process of listening for God's guidance and "resolved *in the Spirit*"[3] that it was necessary to go to Jerusalem, by way of Achaia and Macedonia. One chapter later, Paul will describe his travel plans saying, "And now, compelled *by the Spirit*, I am going to Jerusalem" (Acts 20:22). Paul had spent time laying his plans before God, asking God where he should go. The Spirit had communicated directly to Paul that he should go to Jerusalem.

In each of these examples, God provides specific and direct guidance. It is the same kind (not quality) of guidance that we might receive from a friend, a spouse, or a parent. It is the same kind of guidance that we ourselves might give others. In none of these examples did God respond with moral admonitions or say, "Hey, figure it out for yourself." And in no instance did God refuse to provide counsel (though we will see examples of this in chapter 5).

Hopefully this brief survey of Scripture gives some clarity as to what I mean when I say that God provides us with guidance and counsel. But this raises another question: Just because God clearly guided Rebekah or David or Paul in such a direct way doesn't mean he will do the same for us, does it?

But I'm Not David!

The question of whether stories from the Bible apply to us today can be separated into two questions, one interpretive and one personal. The interpretive question goes something like this: Aren't those passages simply describing what happened in the past, not prescribing what we are to expect in the present? The full answer is best saved for later. For now, suffice it to say that all Scripture, including narratives from the Old Testament, is given by inspiration of God and is profitable for revealing God to us and communicating how God wants us to live today (see 2 Tim. 3:16–17; Rom. 4:23–24; 1 Cor. 10:11).

The second issue is more personal. It goes something like this: of course God guided and directed Saul, Nehemiah, Jesus, and Philip. They were important Bible characters, central to what God is doing in history. But I am not important enough for God to guide me. These stories are about exceptional people and they happen in only exceptional cases, right?

Wrong. Knowing how easy it is for us to fall prey to this kind of thinking, God explicitly tells us otherwise. In James 5:13–16 God wants to encourage ordinary, everyday people like you and me to turn to prayer, so he has James tell a story from the life of Elijah. Anticipating our "But Elijah's important; I'm not!" argument, James continues with, "Elijah was a man just like us" (see v. 17). What is the point of including this phrase? It is to stop us from thinking that God only miraculously intervenes for prophets, priests, and kings.[4] The stories in the Bible do not apply only to extraordinary people. In fact, there are no extraordinary people—just an extraordinary God. God is saying, "Look, they are people just like you. They received my guidance and counsel and so can you."

Likewise, we should not assume God only guides certain Christians, whether the "super mature" or those with some mystical gift of divine GPS or something like that. These verses in James are for all Christians. Besides, in the Old Testament, inquiring of God was something that the average Israelite did (see Exod. 33:7; Judg. 1:1; 1 Sam. 9:9), not just famous Bible characters. More than that, God even guided people who were not members of his covenant people (see Gen. 30:27; 1 Sam. 6:9–12; 2 Chron. 35:21; Matt. 2:12; Acts 10:1–8). God guides people in every different stage of Christian maturity, from the spiritually apathetic to fully devoted followers of Jesus, because God's guidance is for every Christian.

But Does God Care?

But perhaps you might wonder: Does God really care where I go to school? One author put it this way:

> There is no need to sit by the telephone, waiting for God to call. For some reason we assume God has something to say about everything. I'm not sure this is the case. God may remain silent because he has nothing to say. His silence may mean little more than, "Fine, you can be an accountant or a teacher, move to Orlando or stay in Chicago, marry Sam or remain single. It doesn't much matter to me. I'll bless you either way."[5]

In my opinion, this argument takes the wrong approach. Did Dr. Wright care where I went to school? I can't imagine that he did. He had never met me before and would most likely never see me again. He had no personal stake in my decision. Why then did he give me advice? It was an act of Christian kindness. He knew that the decision about which school to attend is a difficult one. He also realized that from his position and experience he had wisdom that was not available to me.

This is where the image in Matthew 7 of God as our Father is so powerful. I referenced this passage earlier, but it is so important that it bears repeating here. Jesus asks,

> Which of you, if his son asks for bread, will give him a stone? Or if he asks for a fish, will give him a snake? If you then, though you are evil, know how to give good gifts to your children, how much more will your Father in heaven give good gifts to those who ask him! (vv. 9–11)

If Tom Wright, who wasn't even my father, was willing in kindness to offer advice, how much more will God, who loves me infinitely, provide counsel and guidance whenever I ask for help?

After all, if Saul was concerned about his lost donkeys, then God was concerned about Saul's lost donkeys (see 1 Sam. 9).

If there is an issue that you need help with—whether where to work, how to handle a stressful situation, what clothes to wear to a job interview, or whatever—and you can think of even one person who might, out of the kindness of their heart, be willing to give you advice on that situation, then surely God will be willing to provide you counsel if you ask.

But isn't one of the goals of parenting to raise children who are able to make decisions for themselves without needing advice? If God is our Father, perhaps his goal is to wean us from depending on his guidance. But I don't think this is right for two reasons. First, it is true that parents should foster independence in their children, but every parent I know still loves to be asked for advice regarding situations of life. My father is eighty-three years old and his face lights up anytime I seek his counsel. As parents we want our children to become independent from parental rules and resources, but not independent from parental counsel.

Second, the analogy to human fathers breaks down when fully applied to God. In reality, Christian parents should not be trying to train their children simply to be independent. They should be trying to transfer their child's dependence to God, because only God is good enough, wise enough, loving enough, and present enough to be completely relied upon. Christian parents know that if their children place their hope in Mom and Dad, they will be ultimately disappointed. But God is always ready, willing, and able to help. The goal of the Christian life is to become more and more dependent upon God.

God cares about the decisions we face because God cares about us.

Is God a Micromanager?

The other end of the spectrum from the mistaken notion that God doesn't care is a picture of God as oppressive when it comes to decisions. At this extreme, I have in mind a micromanaging boss who involves himself in every detail and every decision of our lives. Christians with this distorted picture can become immobilized, fearing that God has one right outfit of clothes for them to wear today and they must pray until they find it. To fail to do so is to fail to obey God. Perhaps we have had a domineering father figure in our lives who treated us this way, or a pastor who ran a church this way, so we think God is like this. Or this view of God may come from mistaken notions inherent in the language of "God's will" that people use to describe what I am talking about here (see the appendix for more on this topic). Whatever the reason, some people believe God wants to micromanage every decision of our lives. If we fail to discover what clothes he wants us to wear today, then we will have stepped outside of his plan for our lives.

But this too is wrong. Paul says defensively in 1 Corinthians 9:3–4, "Don't we have the right to food and drink? Don't we have the right to take a believing wife along with us, as do the other apostles and the Lord's brothers and Cephas?" Paul is free here to make choices in non-moral areas of life without being immobilized by fears of incurring God's wrath for choosing wrongly.

And so are we. Rather than the image of a domineering God who wants to micromanage every decision of our lives, the Bible presents a loving, heavenly Father who loves to provide direct advice and guidance to those who are in need.

But I Have the Mind of Christ!

Some may think, *I don't need this kind of guidance from God because I have the "mind of Christ"* (see 1 Cor. 2:16). By this they mean God guides and directs them through their maturing Christian discernment. As we are conformed to Christ's image, our minds begin to see things the way he sees them. The paths we choose to go down are then the paths that God has chosen for us to go down. There is no need for consciously seeking advice from God and waiting for him to give it.

There is some truth here. As we mature as Christians, there are many thousands of decisions we make without explicitly seeking guidance from God, but which are still influenced by God's Spirit working subtly in and through our maturing spirituality. For example, a man calls on the phone requesting to meet with you to talk about his struggles in his marriage. You don't stop to pray about it because you know helping those in need is the right thing to do. So you agree to meet. This is wholly consistent with the fact that many decisions we see being made in the New Testament are not a matter of God's explicit guidance, but a much more subtle walking in the Spirit.

However, Paul, who introduces us to the notion of having the mind of Christ and being conformed to the image of Christ himself, at times seeks or receives direct counsel and guidance from God (see Acts 13:1–2; 16:6–10; 18:9; 19:21; 20:22–23; 22:17–21; 23:11; 27:23–26; 2 Cor. 12:9; Gal. 2:2). Paul never classifies these overt, explicit interactions with God as being the result of "mature Christian discernment."

Besides, if guidance from God was just another name for having the mind of Christ, why does God use an angel to speak to Peter (see Acts 5:19–20; 12:6–7), Philip (see Acts 8:26), and Paul (see Acts 27:23–26)? Why not just use their mature Christian discernment?

Or consider Jesus. Certainly he has the "mind of Christ." Yet, despite his perfect ability to discern, Jesus is still explicitly guided by the Spirit into the wilderness to be tempted (see Matt. 4:1). When it is time to choose the Twelve, he seeks guidance from his Father (see Luke 6:12). In the struggle of Gethsemane, Jesus asks the Father whether there is some way other than the cross (see Matt. 26:36–46) and receives a negative answer. Jesus does not simply use his perfect discernment in every situation to guide his own steps. There are times he solicits or receives more tangible, direct guidance from the Father or the Holy Spirit.

So while I affirm that in many decisions in life the Spirit leads us more subtly through our growing Christian discernment, this does not eliminate the need for and availability of direct, conscious guidance from God.

Sometimes when I try to explain what I mean by listening for guidance from God, I talk about a godly, wonderful man named Jim Carlson. For the first five years of my job as senior pastor, Jim's office was down the hall from mine. He was twice my age and had forty-five more years of pastoral experience than I had. God had gifted him with great wisdom, deep spirituality, and a real love for me. Anytime I thought I needed advice about work, family, life, or whatever, I knew I could knock on his door and spend time with him, receiving advice and guidance on the issues of life. At other times, Jim would come to me with some unsolicited counsel and advice, helping to steer me down the right paths. While I used my own (hopefully) mature discernment for many decisions, there were times when I needed more explicit guidance or advice, and I would often seek it from Jim.

This is what listening for guidance from God looks like to me. It is the picture of a kind, loving God. He is not dispassionately distant from us, nor is he a domineering micromanager when it comes to the non-moral decisions that make up much of the fabric of our lives. Of course the analogy to Jim is inadequate; after all only God is God, but it does seem to align itself with the most important biblical metaphor God gives when describing his guidance: that of shepherd.

The Good Shepherd

It is no surprise that Jacob, a shepherd and recipient of God's guidance, is the first one in the Bible to introduce the metaphor of God as shepherd (see Gen. 49:24). David, also a shepherd and regular recipient of God's guidance, picks up the theme of God as shepherd and expands it (see Ps. 23), and Ezekiel takes it even further. The metaphor, however, reaches its crescendo on the lips of Jesus, who says of himself as the Good Shepherd: "When he has brought out all his own, he goes on ahead of them, and his sheep follow him because they know his voice" (John 10:4). To understand God's guidance, we must hear what John 10 is saying.

First, God's desire to guide and direct our lives flows out of his deep love for us. In the broader context of John 10, Jesus is talking about how as the Shepherd he lays down his life for the sheep. If God loved us enough to send his Son to die for us, then surely his plan is to give us all things through Jesus (see Rom. 8:32). When we come to ask God for counsel in perplexing situations, we are not twisting his arm or nagging him into submission. He *wants* to lead us; he *longs for* us to recognize his voice. We are his children, the sheep of his pasture (see Ps. 100:3). He *loves* bringing us to green pastures in which to lie down, and leading us beside quiet waters (see Ps. 23:2). This does not mean that God is some cosmic genie ready to guide us to fame and fortune as we command. But it does mean that he wants to lead us to jobs that will bless us, even when they stretch our faith; he revels in helping us find wise spouses and causing us to grow through that process; he longs to show us fulfilling ministry opportunities; he is overjoyed when we seek his counsel in perplexing situations; he desires to show us the paths to take so that we can endure the dark valleys of life.

Second, Jesus actually speaks to us to guide and direct us. In John 10 the sheep do not use their own sheep-smarts to find their way to green pastures and still waters and then call it "the voice of the Shepherd." Guidance from God is not a fancy name for our own wisdom, despite the fact that God does sometimes speak to us through our human wisdom. In addition, the sheep recognize Jesus's voice before they follow him, not simply in retrospect. Some think God's guidance is unknowable until after the fact—and it is true that God can guide us in ways in which we are unaware—but the sheep follow Jesus *because they hear his voice.*

Here then, in John 10, is a beautiful picture of what we are talking about when we speak of God guiding our lives. God is not constantly barking out step-by-step orders to his sheep, nor is he dispassionately disconnected from our daily lives. Instead he is with us, longing to communicate clearly his advice, counsel, and direction for our lives in accordance with our needs.

God Likes Oxford

At the beginning of this chapter, I posed the question: What sort of response should I have expected if I had gone to God and asked him for guidance regarding which school to attend, just like I asked Tom Wright? In fact, I did ask God repeatedly, "What school should I attend?" In response to these prayers, I felt encouraged by God during Tom Wright's lecture to ask Professor Wright's advice. Although he advised me to go to Cambridge, God used his advice as part of a process whereby it became clear what God was telling me to do. God said, "Go to Oxford." (As we will see later, recognizing God's guidance can be a confusing process!)

Discussion Questions

1. Have you ever experienced God giving you a direct answer to a direct question? What were the circumstances, and how did he communicate his answer? How did that impact your relationship with God?

2. After reviewing the examples where God provided direct guidance to people in the Bible, do you feel as if God will speak to you as he spoke to them, or do you feel that these are unique cases? Which of the examples do you most connect with?

3. The image of God as Shepherd is one of the most cherished images in Christianity. How does this image shape your view of God's guidance?

2

why listen for guidance from God?

It is easier not to listen for guidance from God.

When I was twenty-two years old and a brand-new college graduate, my time had finally come to buy my own car, after years of borrowing cars from others. This was the car that would take me into the rest of my life. I felt the weight of this momentous decision. So I summoned my newly acquired analytical skills, discipline, and the impeccable wisdom that only a twenty-two-year-old can have, and threw myself into the process. I researched different car models; I talked to car aficionados; I devoured *Consumer Reports*. Somewhere near the intersection of my dreams and my budget, I zeroed in on a Geo Prizm (a car specifically designed to entice poor, uncool, engineering graduates with an unnatural desire for quality and dependability). Then I began the haggling process, going from dealer to dealer, trying to squeeze every last dollar out of the price of the car. Confident of success, I signed the paperwork and drove off the lot with a brand-new car. I loved my little car.

I kept the car for six years and had almost no problems with it. Not everything about the process of buying a car was enjoyable, but it was rather straightforward. Pick a car, find a dealer, settle on a price, buy the car. Simple. The whole process took roughly three weeks from start to finish.

Nine years later, I was married with two children and one car (sadly not the Geo Prizm!). Our family needed another car, yet taking on a new car payment would have been quite a financial burden. What should we do? By this time my impeccable twenty-two-year-old wisdom had given way to a more healthy thirty-one-year-old humility about making decisions. During the intervening nine years I had experienced more and more guidance from God. So this time I decided to approach car buying differently. Instead of simply choosing using human wisdom, I would seek counsel from the Lord. I sought the Lord earnestly and asked him if we should buy another car. Months went by. No answer came. I did nothing rather than make a decision on my own. It was painful to wait. As a husband and father, I felt that I was letting my family down, and hated watching my wife sacrifice to make our one-car situation work. However, after five months of praying, my wife's brother, Andrew, moved in with us, bringing his well-worn car with him. This seemed to be God's way of telling us not to buy a car and to make do with borrowing Andrew's car on occasion. It was not my preferred answer, but it was an answer.

A few months later, however, Andrew's car died. "What are we supposed to do now?" I asked the Lord. It was very frustrating. We had been asking God for specific guidance for more than seven months. At times we had no idea what God was saying. There was more waiting than I imagined there would be.

Two experiences buying a car. The first was straightforward with little stress and not much time required. The second was much more confusing, quite stressful, and dragged out much longer.

So why would anyone seek direct guidance from the Lord when it is so much easier to decide for ourselves? Why pursue advice from God, when we can use rational logic or "gut feeling" intuition and make the decisions on our own?

Shouldn't People Ask God for Guidance?

The main reason we should seek guidance from the Lord is that he *encourages us to do so*. This encouragement is evident in the Scriptures in a number of ways, but one of the most memorable is an epitaph God wrote to commemorate the burial of Saul, the first king of Israel.

> Saul died because he was unfaithful to the LORD; he did not keep the word of the LORD and even consulted a medium for guidance, *and did not inquire of the LORD*. So the LORD put him to death and turned the kingdom over to David son of Jesse (1 Chron. 10:13–14, emphasis mine).

God highlights Saul's two most devastating failures as warnings to us. First, Saul did not keep the word of the Lord. No surprise that God was angry with him for that. The second catches most people off-guard. Saul did not "inquire of the Lord." Essentially God was angry with Saul because Saul did not seek guidance from him, choosing instead to rely on his own decision-making abilities.[1]

Unfortunately the nation of Israel, for the most part, did not heed the warning of Saul's epitaph. Later, in the era of the prophets, God would repeatedly complain about Israel failing to listen for his guidance. "Is it because there is no God in Israel that you are going off to consult Baal-Zebub the god of Ekron?" (2 Kings 1:3); "The shepherds are senseless and do not inquire of the LORD, so they do not prosper and all their flock is scattered" (Jer. 10:21); "[I will cut off] those who turn back from following the LORD, and neither seek the LORD, nor inquire of him" (Zeph. 1:6); "They set up kings without my consent, they choose princes without my approval" (Hosea 8:4).

The motivation from these negative indictments is buttressed by positive affirmations that God wants to lead and guide us. What else are we to conclude when God presents himself as the one who guided Abraham to a new land (see Gen. 12:1); the one who led Israel out of Egypt to the Promised Land through a pillar of fire (see Exod. 13:21–22); the one who commanded Joshua and the nation to follow the Ark into the Promised Land because "then you will know which way to go, since you have never been this way before" (Josh. 3:3–4); the one whom David praises for leading and guiding him (see Pss. 23:2–3; 73:24; 139:10) and prays to for such guidance (see Ps. 31:3)? When God tells us that through the Spirit he led Simeon into the temple courts to see Jesus (see Luke 2:25–27), sent Jesus into the wilderness to be tempted by Satan (see Matt. 4:1), led Peter to go speak in the temple court (see Acts 5:20), and brought Philip to the side of the Ethiopian's chariot (see Acts 8:29)—should we not think that God is encouraging us to listen for his guiding voice?

Add to that the fact that God directly encourages us to seek his guidance. In the Old Testament God says,

> Someone may say to you, "Let's ask the mediums and those who consult the spirits of the dead. With their whisperings and mutterings, they will tell us what to do." But shouldn't people ask God for guidance? Should the living seek guidance from the dead? (Isa. 8:19 NLT)

In the New Testament God is even more direct, saying, "If any of you lacks wisdom, you should ask God, who gives generously to all without finding fault, and it will be given to you" (James 1:5).[2] The main reason we listen for guidance from God is that he encourages us to do so.

A Better Guide

So God encourages us to listen for his guidance. Why? Because he is a better guide for our lives than we are.

We all know people who are poor decision makers. Maybe it is a child who constantly chooses the wrong type of friends, a group of business leaders who seem to make irrational and uninformed business decisions, a church board that refuses to embrace exciting ministry opportunities, a parent who makes choices that waste money and time, a friend who keeps hopping from job to job, or a sibling who lets your nieces and nephews experience too much too quickly.

But what about us? Am I a good decision maker? Are you? I'd like to think that I am, but current research doesn't support my claim. According to Richard Thaler, the director of the Center for Decision Research at the University of Chicago, careful research by social scientists over the past four decades has raised serious questions about the rationality of many judgments and decisions that all of us make.[3] This conclusion has been confirmed by others in the fields of behavioral economics and psychology. For example, a recent *New York Times* bestseller entitled *Sway: The Irresistible Pull of Irrational Behavior* is built on the thesis that, "Although most of us think of ourselves as rational, we're much more prone to irrational behavior than we realize."[4] Dan Ariely, a behavioral economics professor at Duke University, argues for this exact point in *Predictably Irrational: The Hidden Forces That Shape Our Decisions.*[5] Shai Danzinger, Jonathan Levav, and Liora Avnaim-Pesso, researchers at Ben Gurion and Columbia Universities, provided a recent headline-grabbing example of the same trend when they found that judicial decisions were not only a function of rational legal reasoning but also how long ago the judge's last break was.[6] Tobias Moskowitz and Jon Wertheim did the same when they discovered that home-field advantage in sports is a result of officials being unwittingly influenced in their decisions by the home crowd.[7]

This is nothing new. Ever since Adam and Eve decided to eat the fruit God commanded them not to eat, smart humans have been making bad decisions. Solomon is a perfect case in point. Solomon, the wisest of men, made some colossally dumb decisions such as allowing himself to be seduced into idolatry by his hundreds of wives and stockpiling horses when God told him not to.

When we are humbled by our own shortcomings and failures in guiding our own lives, we are ready to listen for God's guidance. Charles Spurgeon says it this way, commenting on Psalm 73:

> The Psalmist felt his need of divine guidance. He had just been discovering the foolishness of his own heart, and lest he should be constantly led astray by it, he resolved that God's counsel should henceforth guide him. A sense of our own folly is a great step toward being wise, when it leads us to rely on the wisdom of the Lord. The blind man leans on his friend's arm and reaches home in safety, and so would we give ourselves up implicitly to divine guidance, nothing doubting; assured that though we cannot see, it is always safe to trust the all-seeing God.[8]

Let me share five reasons why God is a better guide for our lives than we are.

God Knows Our True Motives

Dan Ariely, the author of *Predictably Irrational*, tells his own story of buying a car: "When I turned thirty, I decided it was time to trade in my motorcycle for a car, but I could not decide which car was right for me. The web was just taking off and to my delight, I found a site that provided advice on purchasing cars." Professor Ariely describes how he answered all of the questions on the website, which then recommended that he purchase a Ford Taurus. He describes his reaction this way:

> The problem was that, having just surrendered my motorcycle, I couldn't see myself driving a sedate sedan. I was now facing a dilemma: I had tried a deliberative and thoughtful process for my car selection and I didn't like the answer I got. So, I did what I think anyone in my position would do. I hit the BACK button a few times, backtracked to earlier stages of the interview

process, and changed many of my original answers to what I convinced myself were more accurate and appropriate responses. . . . I kept this up until the car-advertising website suggested a Mazda Miata. The moment the program was kind enough to recommend a small convertible, I felt grateful for the fantastic software and decided to follow its advice.

Commenting on what he learned in the process, Professor Ariely says, "The experience taught me that sometimes we want our decisions to have a rational veneer when, in fact, they stem from a gut feeling—what we crave deep down."[9]

If I were to rephrase Professor Ariely's discovery in biblical terms, it would be Proverbs 16:2–3: "All a person's ways seem innocent to them, but motives are weighed by the LORD. Commit to the LORD whatever you do, and he will establish your plans." The success of our decisions is based on our motivations for making those decisions. Unfortunately, we often think our motives are pure, but they are easily contaminated by the world's values, as well as our own personal preferences and cravings.

Many people have chosen a career because it will please (or spite) their parents. Many have chosen a spouse for the same reason. Some choose to go into ministry because of a deep-seated longing to be needed. A friend of mine switched companies ostensibly to spend more time with his family, but ended up with a higher paying job that caused him to be gone from home even more. A college student decided not to play a favorite sport in college in order to focus on studies, but later admitted it was in part because of a fear of not making the team. Pride, greed, fear, laziness, and selfishness all lurk within the recesses of our hearts. Who can know which of these are poisoning our motives and subtly sabotaging our decisions?

But what is hidden to us is clear to God. The thoughts and attitudes of all humans are laid open before him (see Heb. 4:12–13). When we turn to the Lord for counsel and guidance, he can reveal to us our motivations. Even more powerfully, when we empty ourselves of our own desires and allow God to guide us, our own motivations become a non-factor. For example, one

March day a woman named Sharon came to me and said she was feeling prompted by God to share her story with others. For twenty years she had kept quiet, fearing that if people really knew what she had been through and what she had done they would reject her. Yet God had been prying open the recesses of her heart and shining his healing light into the solitude of darkness. She now wanted to help others, but was leaving it in our hands to decide what the appropriate time and place were.

Independently, women close to Sharon had been praying for her about this same thing. They could see what God was doing in her life and knew that she needed to testify about it. According to them, Easter Sunday morning was the day God was impressing on them for this to happen. I sensed they had truly received guidance from God, so we arranged for Sharon to share her story on that morning.

How did Sharon know that she wasn't sharing on Easter Sunday morning because she secretly longed for the attention such a platform could bring? Or how could she be sure that deep down she wasn't craving sympathy from others? Testifying to God's grace is always the right thing to do, but it is possible to manipulate the times and places to glorify ourselves in the process. How could Sharon know that latent impure motives were not driving her decision to share?

Because she hadn't been in control of the process! God was the one working behind the scenes, leading and guiding through other people. If Sharon had campaigned for the opportunity to speak, her unknown motives might have sabotaged her. By allowing God to lead and guide, she was confident that her motivation was pure as she stood there on that Easter Sunday morning, sharing what God had done in her life.

God Can Navigate through Competing Values

Some decisions in life are agonizingly complex. In the midst of a recession, a Christian business owner may face a difficult choice. Should he lay off good, loyal workers to make the company more financially viable in the short term, or should he try to weather the storm even if it means accepting more financial liability to do so? In this example, good Christian values are in conflict: on one hand, the values of mercy and rewarding loyalty; on the other hand, good stewardship and a desire to provide jobs for the remaining workers into the future.

Or consider the case of aging parents living in their own home. On one hand, you want to respect their ability to make decisions; on the other hand, you want to ensure their safety. The biblical command to honor parents is clear enough, but does this mean respecting their right to make their own decisions before the Lord (see Rom. 14) or stepping in to help those who cannot help themselves (see 1 Tim. 5:16)? And if moving to an assisted living arrangement is best, how hard do you push?

Or imagine a woman whose husband has been repeatedly unfaithful. According to Matthew 19 she is allowed to divorce him, but should she? Would it be better to continue to stay in the marriage, following the example of God in his relationship with the southern kingdom of Judah (see Hosea 1)? Or should she divorce him, following God's example with the northern kingdom of Israel (see Jer. 3)?

The complexity of this last example came home to me as I sat in my office looking into the tearful face of a wife who, over a number of years, had been the victim of repeated acts of infidelity. Besides the obvious shame, pain, and devastation, she was thoroughly confused. Should she divorce her husband? On one hand, she wanted to shield her children and herself from his damaging, sinful choices. On the other hand, she knew that God could work through grace and forgiveness to bring about the transformation that her husband needed. She believed that she had received mercy and grace from God and was obligated to show that to others, including her husband. But she also believed that God hates sin and disciplines those who recklessly engage in such sinful acts. What was she to do? Almost every person she knew had an opinion, and almost universally they were urging her to divorce him. Yet God guided her to stay in her marriage. She never did tell me how he communicated this to her, but she was sure. I do admit, at the time, secretly thinking she had misheard God. I was wrong, though. Miraculously, God used her sacrificial, long-suffering love to bring her husband—who had been claiming to be a Christian all along—to true faith. I thank the Lord she was willing to listen to God as he guided her through this moral maze.

Our most difficult decisions are often not between right and wrong, but between right and right. The confusion of competing values makes many decisions inordinately complex, and it can be impossible to know for certain the best course of action without some outside help. Yet Jesus makes such decisions with ease, as he demonstrated in Matthew 12 when his disciples were caught between the competing values of needing food and honoring the Sabbath. We do well to listen for his counsel when we find ourselves in similarly confusing situations.

God Is Not Overwhelmed by Options

Studies have shown that people are easily overwhelmed as their number of choices increases.[10] While most times we are glad for increased opportunities to choose, too much choice immobilizes and confuses us. We use common strategies to narrow down our choices, but this invariably leads to errors in decision making.[11]

The complexity of simple decisions that we all make regularly at, say, the grocery store, only highlights the complexity of decisions that really matter. Take, for example, finding a spouse. In an earlier era, people tended to have smaller spheres of life. Perhaps they lived their whole lives in the same small town. As a result their number of potential spouses was quite limited. Today, however, we are connected to the world. Our participation in the global village means an exponential increase in the amount of choice. Fifty years ago it was rather improbable that a young man from rural America would meet—let alone marry—a young Christian woman from China. Today it is not uncommon. Yet who is competent to choose among the millions of potential spouses in the world? How can you properly decide whether you should marry the young man you are currently dating in college or wait until you move to Mexico City after graduation, where you will be exposed to a whole new world of people? What assurance is there that the next person you meet on the online dating service won't be a better match?

Not only are there more choices now, we are bombarded with more information to consider when making a choice. Think again about selecting a spouse. Singles are told to consider a future spouse's family history, personality type, love language, family of origin, career goals, sexual history, childrearing philosophies, financial issues, psychological health, abusive tendencies, and so much more. Who can make such a decision? Sure, we can just throw caution to the wind, not over-think it, and go with our gut feelings. But who can vouch for how successful that decision is going to be? (I am not claiming that the success of a marriage rides solely on the initial decision, but the initial decision is certainly a factor.)

The famous poet T. S. Eliot once insightfully commented: "Where is the wisdom we have lost in knowledge and the knowledge that we have lost in information?"[12] Eliot's point is that wisdom—and our ability to make wise decisions—is being overwhelmed by an ever-growing tidal wave of knowledge and information.

While we cannot process all the possible choices in life, God knows what would happen even in hypothetical situations (see Matt. 11:21). Whereas we cannot master all the relevant information, God has even numbered the hairs of our heads (see Matt. 10:30). God is not overwhelmed by choices or information.

We see this exemplified in God's choice of David to be the second king of Israel. Sending Samuel directly to Jesse's house, God tells him not to select any of the brothers present because God sees into their hearts. Undeterred by the fact that Jesse seems to be out of sons, Samuel insists there must be another one somewhere. Finding David, Samuel is told by God to anoint him king.

Can you imagine, however, if Samuel had to find the next king without God's help? How many men would he have had to interview to get to the youngest son of a family in one of the smallest clans in Judah? Even if he could somehow interview all of the men in Israel, Samuel would never have been able to see into their hearts to decide who had the right qualifications to be king. Finding David was like finding a needle in a haystack. But God handles such decisions with ease.

God Knows What We Cannot

Too many of our decisions are based on information that later turns out to be wrong. I've used the example of buying a car multiple times in this chapter. So, suppose you decided to purchase a Toyota in late 2009, based in part on their impeccable quality and safety record. If you had done so, you would have been in for a rude awakening in early 2010 when Toyota began to recall millions of cars because of quality and safety issues. For those of us who grew up hearing mythical tales of Toyota's quality, this was unfathomable. In March 2010, CNN's website reported that Toyota had informed dealers as early as 2002 about safety concerns with some of their cars. The lawyer interviewed in the article claimed that Toyota and the National Highway Traffic Safety Administration hid this information from the public.[13] By 2010, Toyota's quality and safety problems were well known to the public, but if you had bought a car in 2009, you would have already made your decision to purchase a Toyota, perhaps in part on the basis of wrong information.

Likewise, we are often victims of hidden forces trying to affect our decisions. In 1957 Vance Packard wrote a highly influential book called *The Hidden Persuaders* that showed how marketing, advertising, and public relations people were using psychological insights to influence decisions about what we buy and for whom we vote.[14] If this was true in the 1950s it is even more true today. Richard Thaler and Cass Sunstein's book *Nudge* begins with a study of how children's eating decisions in a cafeteria are highly impacted by which foods the cafeteria manager chooses to place at eye-level and near the cash register. There is, after all, a reason why grocery stores force you to walk through an aisle of candy in order to check out! These are simple examples, but they open our eyes to see that there are shrewd people in this world who attempt to manipulate the decisions we make by taking advantage of our naiveté and inexperience. And I haven't even mentioned Satan, the great deceiver, who works night and day to trip us up in the decisions we make.

When we don't even know whether the information on which we are basing our decisions is correct, and when we don't understand the forces attempting to influence our decisions, what hope do we have of making effective decisions?

In the beginning of the book of Joshua, the Israelites are sweeping through the Promised Land. With their victories at Jericho and Ai, word began to spread about this invading horde. Most of the people groups west of the Jordan decided to band together to fight Israel, but the Gibeonites chose a different strategy, resorting to a ruse. Loading their donkeys with worn-out clothes, cracked wineskins, and moldy bread, the Gibeonites sent a delegation to Israel. Upon arrival after their short trip, the delegation announced to Joshua and Israel, "We have come from a distant country; make a treaty with us."

The men of Israel responded, "But perhaps you live near us. How then can we make a treaty with you?"

"This bread of ours was warm when we packed it at home on the day we left to come to you. But now see how dry and moldy it is. And these wineskins that we filled were new, but see how cracked they are. And our clothes and sandals are worn out by the very long journey."

Believing their lies, the Israelites made a treaty with Gibeon, only to discover three days later that they had been tricked. By then it was too late. They could not attack Gibeon because of the treaty that they had signed. Joshua 9:14 gives us a post-mortem on the decision-making process: "The men of Israel sampled their provisions *but did not inquire of the* LORD." The point wasn't that Israel didn't do due diligence. They checked the evidence as best they could. There was no way for them, humanly speaking, to know that the evidence had been falsified. The author of Joshua almost wistfully adds, "if only they had asked the LORD."

When Abraham tricked Abimelech into thinking Sarah was not his wife, it was the Lord who guided Abimelech to the right decision despite the deception (see Gen. 20). When David couldn't figure out why there had been a famine for three years in the land, he sought the face of the Lord God, who told him it was a result of something that had happened years ago during the reign of the previous king (see 2 Sam. 21:1). When Daniel was faced with the unknowable question of what the king had dreamt, he pled for counsel from the Lord, who gave it (see Dan. 2:18). When Ananias and Sapphira lied to the early church, the Holy Spirit told Peter what he could not know on his own (see Acts 5:1–11). When the elders of our church were asked to determine whether an incredibly gifted liar was indeed as repentant for his sins as he claimed, they begged God to reveal to them what no one else had been able to determine, and God clearly did.

God knows what we cannot know, and wants to guide our lives in accordance with his knowledge.

God Will Guide Us toward Future Joy

We all are aware that things can go wrong in the future, shipwrecking the best-laid plans. We may decide to be a teacher only to find when we graduate that teaching jobs are in short supply. We may find the perfect home only to be denied credit because of newly passed lending guidelines. We may choose to begin a family only to discover that we are not physically able to have children.

But consider the problem of the future from a different point of view. What if every decision worked out exactly the way we had hoped and dreamed? Would we be pleased? Daniel Gilbert, a psychology professor at Harvard University, has written a stimulating book called *Stumbling on Happiness* in which he uses some of the latest research in the social sciences to show that because we are not good at predicting what will make us happy in the future, we make poor decisions in the present.[15]

Jewel Whitakker would readily agree with Gilbert's findings. In 2002 her husband Jack won the then-largest Powerball Lottery jackpot in history: $314 million (the one-time payment after taxes equaled $114 million). A dream come true, right? Not quite. By 2004 Jewel was in a place she would not have imagined in her worst nightmares. Because of the money, a series of terrible tragedies befell their beloved granddaughter, culminating in her tragic death. Jewel was reported as saying that "she wished her husband had never won the lottery. If she had known what was ahead, 'I would've torn up that ticket.' "[16]

A wise man once told me to be careful what I wished for—because I just might get it. Because we don't know the future, we are flying blind in the present. We cannot navigate our way to future joy.

The same is not true of God. That is why Jeremiah 29:11 says, " 'I know the plans I have for you,' declares the LORD, 'plans to prosper you and not to harm you, plans to give you hope and a future.' " These words speak of a God who is willing and able to navigate those he loves toward a joyful, peaceful, hopeful future. God is better equipped to guide us in life because through his guidance he draws us closer to himself. We experience a deeper relationship with God and as a result joy, peace, and hope.

That is why, speaking in the context of God's unfathomable love for us, Ephesians 3:20 says, "now unto him who is able to do immeasurably more than all *we can ask or imagine*" (emphasis mine). The very best that we can imagine for ourselves and our future pales in comparison to what God can (and wants to) do for us.

This verse in Ephesians reminds me of the conversation Han Solo and Luke Skywalker had in *Star Wars: A New Hope*. Luke is trying to convince Han Solo to help rescue Princess Leia, and the conversation goes something like this:

Luke Skywalker: "Listen, if you were to rescue her, the reward would be . . ."
Han Solo: "What?"
Luke Skywalker: "Well, more wealth than you can imagine."
Han Solo: "I don't know, I can imagine quite a bit."

We are sure that God can't really do more than we can imagine, because we can dream up scenarios where we are inordinately wealthy, powerful, beautiful, or successful. Yet that is not ultimately what God wants for us. What he wants for us is infinite joy. C. S. Lewis says it this way, "We are half-hearted creatures, fooling about with drink and sex and ambition when infinite joy is offered us, like an ignorant child who wants to go on making mud pies in a slum because he cannot imagine what is meant by the offer of a holiday at the sea. We are far too easily pleased."[17]

Stop and imagine yourself in the most joyful future possible. What do you see in your mind's eye? Where are you living? What are you doing with your time? How many children and grandchildren do you have, and what does your relationship look like with them? What are the accomplishments of your life? What are the valleys that God will have brought you through? What surprises will have come your way in life? Who are your closest friends and companions? Even more difficult to imagine: When you stand before Jesus on the day of judgment, what will be your glory and your joy?

It is easy to picture what wealth and worldly success might look like for us in the future, but it is hard to imagine joy. How then can we chart our course to ensure that we end up at joy? Many have pursued money and power and ended up joyless and bitter. Many have steered their lives exactly where they wanted to go, only to find themselves miserable upon arrival.

This is ultimately where our wisdom and discernment fail us. We cannot even picture where we should go, let alone know how to get there. But God knows.

Thinking to Yourself vs. Inquiring of God

The wisdom of seeking guidance from God and the folly of trusting in our own abilities is what animates the famous verses from Proverbs 3: "Trust in the LORD with all your heart and lean not on your own understanding; in all your ways submit to him, and he will make your paths straight" (vv. 5–6). The wisest thing Proverbs teaches us is not to trust human wisdom.

This is illustrated beautifully in 1 Samuel 27. Up until that point in David's life, God's guidance shone in and through the decisions that David made. Chapter 27, however, begins ominously.

> But David thought to himself, "One of these days I will be destroyed by the hand of Saul. The best thing I can do is to escape to the land of the Philistines. Then Saul will give up searching for me anywhere in Israel, and I will slip out of his hand." (v. 1)

Here, for the first time in David's narrative the emphasis is placed on his own rational reasoning. The wording "thought to himself" is so natural to us that we don't realize it has never before appeared (or will again) in David's story. This is not a positive comment. It means David did not seek the Lord's guidance. Instead he "thought to himself" and determined the "best thing I can do."

As the story unfolds it looks like he's made a good decision. 1 Samuel 27:4 says, "When Saul was told that David had fled to Gath, he no longer searched for him." Exactly what David predicted would happen! The problem, however, was that something happened he didn't predict that pierced his heart. One day, upon returning to their homes in Philistine territory, David and his men found that the city had been burned to the ground. All their women and children had been carried off in a raid. David's "wisdom" had led his men out of the frying pan and into the fire. First Samuel 30:4, 6 records, "David and his men wept aloud until they had no strength left to weep. . . . David was greatly distressed because the men were talking of stoning him; each one was bitter in spirit because of his sons and daughters." (I am sure they wept for their wives too.)

This is David relying on his own wisdom.

Give David credit, though. He's a quick learner. Verse 6 continues with "But David found strength in the LORD." So what does he do next? Does he sit down and think to himself about what to do? No. Immediately David summons Abiathar the priest, asking for the provisions to be able to inquire of the Lord. "Shall I pursue this raiding party? Will I overtake them?" David asked. "Pursue them," God answered. "You will certainly overtake them and succeed" (see vv. 7–8).

And he did.

This is a perfect illustration of what Proverbs 3:5–6 is saying. In the first decision David leaned on his own understanding. In the second one, he trusted the Lord to lead and guide him.

This is why we seek guidance from God.

More Than I Could Have Ever Asked or Imagined

Having made the case that of the two options for guidance in decision making—ourselves or God—God is the better option, let me remind you that I began this chapter by saying it is easier to choose not to seek guidance from God. I want to be very frank and honest, and affirm once again that this is the more difficult road. Seeking guidance from God can at times be incredibly frustrating, because when we look to the Lord for counsel we are no longer in control of the process. We can't force God to give us guidance in the way we want it to come—or when we want it to arrive. We can't make it unambiguously clear in the way that we want it to be unambiguously clear.[18]

Yet I am reminded that although looking to God for guidance is the harder road, it is always the better road. Earlier, I compared looking for a new car using human wisdom with looking to God for guidance. Making a decision using my own wisdom in the first case was easier, but I have to tell you that there was nothing special about the car I ended up with. In the second case, where I sought guidance from God, the process was much longer and more difficult. However, one Monday in the middle of November, after praying earnestly for God to show us what to do, we received a phone call from dear friends of ours. They informed us that they were buying a new car. I was genuinely glad for them and began to congratulate them. But the husband continued, "We were going to trade in our old minivan to the dealer," he said. "But we felt compelled that we should give it to you instead. Would you be interested?" I was overjoyed at the prospect of getting a car that would meet our family's needs—and for free! While it was a used car, it was in excellent condition, and was nicer than any we would have been able to buy on our own. To date we have had the car for six years and 50,000 miles.

Yet that is not all. Two days later when I walked into my office, a kindhearted man from our church was waiting for me. "Come on," he said. "We are going to Berger Chevrolet." Relishing the confusion written across my silent face, he smiled and added, "You've got a new car to pick up." Almost speechless, I explained to him how just two days earlier God had provided for our needs. My friend smiled again. "Apparently God is giving you two cars this week." We then got into his car and drove to the dealer. There waiting for me was a brand-new Equinox. Again, although a relatively modest vehicle, it was a nicer car than I had ever owned and far beyond what our monthly budget would have allowed at the time.

Two free cars in one week! It is still hard to believe. We passed our previous car on to my brother-in-law. Suddenly everyone living in our house had a new car. If we had followed our human wisdom and bought a car when the need arose, we would have missed out on all of this. By seeking guidance from God, we endured a much more difficult decision-making process but ended up with a far, far better result.

Does this mean that when we seek guidance from God everything has a storybook ending? Not at all. Jesus listens to the Father and ends up with Judas Iscariot as one of his disciples. Polycarp listens to God and is led to martyrdom. Even in the case of these two cars, we have had problems. But I can testify that even when God has led us down difficult paths, his guidance has always been better than anything I could ever have imagined.

Why listen for guidance from God? Because God wants and is able to guide our lives down paths beyond what we could ever imagine or achieve on our own, drawing us ever closer to him in the process.

Discussion Questions

1. Do you consider yourself a good decision maker? What process do you use to make decisions?

2. In this chapter, I shared five reasons why God is a better decision maker than we are. Which of these reasons do you most resonate with? Are there any additional reasons God is better at making decisions than we are?

3. Have there been any decisions you have made that have convinced you of your need for guidance from God?

3

how does God speak to us?

Whenever I share these thoughts about God leading and guiding us, I am invariably asked two questions. One: But *how* does God speak to us to guide and direct? Two: How do you *know* it is God speaking and not someone or something else? Hands down, these are the most common questions I am asked. Perhaps these questions, or ones like them, have already begun to formulate in your mind.

Let's begin with the first question: How does God communicate his guidance and direction? Two truths must be held in tension as we try to answer this question. First, God is *mysterious*. His thoughts are above our thoughts and his ways are above our ways (see Isa. 55:8). There is no mechanical formula he follows when communicating with us. I cannot give you a three-step process for how God will speak to you. God doesn't follow three-step processes. There is a mystery to exactly how God communicates. This, however, must be balanced with a second truth about God. Namely, God is *consistent*. While we cannot predict exactly how he will communicate, he always acts in accordance with who he is and how he has acted in the past. Hebrews 13:7–8 says,

"Remember your leaders, who spoke the word of God to you. Consider the outcome of their way of life and imitate their faith. Jesus Christ is the same yesterday and today and forever." By looking at ways God has communicated guidance and council to others in the past, we can be confident that God will use these ways again to communicate guidance today.

With that in mind, let me show you twelve different ways that God has used to communicate with his people. Each one is attested by Scripture and confirmed by human experience.

The Bible

It was early Monday morning, June 21, 2010. A few days earlier, I had begun to work on the second chapter of this book. Having taught the material many times, I was confident regarding the organization of the chapter. Now I needed to actually start writing. Following the Bible reading program at our church, I began the morning of June 21 by reading Proverbs 21. I dutifully read each verse, sleepily progressing in a halfhearted way toward the end of the chapter. When I reached verse 22, however, it reached out and grabbed me. Suddenly I was fully awake and completely focused. I felt positive that God was speaking directly to me through this verse. I had been praying and asking God to guide me in general as I wrote. Now God was speaking: "A wise man attacks the city of the mighty and pulls down the stronghold in which they trust" (Prov. 21:22 NIV 1984). My mind began to race. In the past, I had only ever focused on the benefits of seeking guidance from God. But on that day, through that passage, I felt God saying to me that I should first attack the stronghold in which we as decision makers place our trust. Before we are ready to seek guidance from God, we have to be convinced that we are not the best source of guidance for our own lives. Here is what I wrote in my prayers that morning:

Lord, the Proverb today: a wise man attacks the city of the mighty, he pulls down the stronghold in which they trust—is

You telling me in the chapter to first demolish human confidence in our own decision making process so that we might be able to establish confidence in You, Lord, as decision maker, isn't it?

By way of confirmation, that same day I went into a Christian bookstore to get a commentary, and there staring me straight in the face was *Stumbling on Happiness*, a book about why we are not as good at making decisions as we think we are! The fact that the book was prominently displayed was odd because (1) it is not a Christian book, (2) it seemed to be the only copy they had, and (3) it was in the new arrivals section even though it was four years old. Staring at that book, it dawned on me that I had just finished reading a similar book, *Predictably Irrational*. I realized that God was now tying these experiences together and using Proverbs 21:22 to give me clear guidance as to how to approach what I was working on.

God's Word is often described as providing guidance and direction. For example, the psalmist says: "Your word is a lamp for my feet, a light on my path" (Ps. 119:105). Such passages are usually talking first and foremost about how God's clear moral instruction in his Word illuminates the choice between right and wrong. Additionally, though, these passages imply that God will use his Word to communicate guidance and direction with regard to non-moral decisions as he speaks through different passages into our lives. It is quite common for God to take a particular passage of the Bible, like he did with me and Proverbs 21:22, and speak through the text into our lives by applying that text to a particular situation.

Take the more drastic example of Brother Yun, a persecuted Chinese Christian. In 1981, the first time Brother Yun experienced persecution for preaching the gospel, he found himself lying on the wet ground in the middle of the night crying out to God for counsel: "Why are they treating us like this? Why can't you protect us?" God responded to his cry for guidance by bringing to mind 1 Peter 2:21 and Isaiah 30:20–21, using these texts to directly answer Brother Yun's questions and encourage his heart.[1]

Let me offer one more example, since this is the most common and important way that God speaks to us. Two weeks before Easter, our church leadership was facing a monumental decision. For three years we had been working toward planting a church in an area of the city that desperately needed one. God appeared to have provided a church planter, a core group, and a vision for reaching this neighborhood. However, we had been working at this for three years and didn't have much fruit to show for it. We knew it would be a struggle, but the process had been much more difficult than we ever imagined. The obstacles going forward seemed insurmountable. The drain on our resources would be immense—resources that could be used to do other important kingdom work. Had we misheard God? Should we pull the plug on this endeavor, or go ahead and try to launch? The stakes were huge. We couldn't afford to make a wrong decision.

One deacon at our church was one of the leaders having the most serious doubts. Feeling the oppressive weight of this decision, this deacon woke up at 5:00 a.m. on Wednesday morning, ten days before Easter, to beg God for guidance. That was the day he was supposed to meet with the church planter and tell him whether or not he thought the church plant should continue. Although anxious to dive right into praying, he felt compelled to do his Bible reading for the day first. So he opened to his reading for the day. It was Luke 13. Stunned, he read:

> A man had a fig tree growing in his vineyard, and he went to look for fruit on it but did not find any. So he said to the man who took care of the vineyard, "For three years now I've been coming to look for fruit on this fig tree and haven't found any. Cut it down! Why should it use up the soil?"
>
> "Sir," the man replied, "leave it alone for one more year, and I'll dig around it and fertilize it. If it bears fruit next year, fine! If not, then cut it down." (vv. 6–9)

Three years, little fruit, the prospect of wasting valuable resources—it was as if this parable had been written for our situation. The deacon called me. "I think I know what God wants us to do," he said. He directed me to Luke 13. As I read the passage, my jaw dropped. Had this parable always been there? It was like I had never seen this passage of Scripture before. Was this not God telling us to give the church plant another year?

God speaks regularly and consistently through his Word. Let me show you a variation of this idea, unique enough to deserve its own category.

The Preached Word

Sitting in a dark room doing video editing, JP heard his phone begin to ring. It was his dad. The news was not good. While JP and his family had known for some time that his dad had inoperable cancer, they had originally been told he could expect about another three years to live. Now his dad was calling with the gut-wrenching news: the doctors had changed their prediction. What was once three years had been revised down to three months.

When JP got off the phone with his dad, he immediately called his wife. What should they do? JP was in his final semester of graduate school, a long way from home. Should he quit school and move home immediately? Should he try to finish the final semester and hope his dad could hang on? But what if JP couldn't get a job in his hometown? What if his father defied expectations and lived longer than expected? Together he and his wife immediately began searching for God's leading.

Talking together, they recounted what had happened a month and a half earlier. At that point JP and Stephanie had been trying to decide whether they needed to move back home after graduation to be with JP's dad as he faced his battle with cancer. One Sunday, while JP and Stephanie were in the midst of waiting for guidance from God, they found themselves sitting in a church service where the pastor was preaching from 1 Corinthians 10:13, a comforting promise that God will never give us more than we can bear. At the end of his sermon, the pastor began using a fictional story about a person whom God allowed to be diagnosed with inoperable cancer, having no idea that JP and Stephanie were in the congregation. In his illustration the pastor told how God arranged to have a child move home to help take care of the dying parent. At that moment, JP and Stephanie both felt God was saying this story was specifically for them. They were to move home after graduation.

Now, having received the bad news that JP's dad only had a few months to live, they reviewed the guidance they had received a month and half earlier. With much prayer and discernment, JP and Stephanie concluded that God was not only telling them to move home after graduation, but he had anticipated this turn of events and, as they reflected again on the sermon, they determined he was telling them to move home immediately. They did. JP was able to spend wonderful time with his dad for a couple of months, and then his father passed into eternity.

The sermon was the means God used to speak to them. When we gather together for worship as the church, God is uniquely present in our midst, especially during the preaching of the Word of God. During this time, God often speaks in powerful ways, communicating guidance and direction to his people.

For myself, I remember sitting in a church service listening to my pastor, Ed Dobson, preach a sermon on Luke 6:12–16. In that passage Jesus prays all night before choosing the twelve apostles. That passage and that sermon stuck with me. I couldn't get it out of my head. Just a short time after that, Lisa and I moved overseas so I could begin doctoral studies. Having stepped out on faith, I wanted nothing more than for God to choose a research project for me. As I was wondering how to go about hearing from him, God kept bringing that sermon on Luke 6:12–16 to my mind. The thought that kept bouncing around in my head was that if Jesus spent all night asking God to select twelve apostles for him, then surely I needed to spend all night in prayer asking God for a research topic. This was God speaking to me through a sermon.

Individual Prayer (and Fasting)

Luke 6:12–16 reminds us that God provides counsel not only *in response to* our prayers, but also sometimes *during* our prayers. Such prayers are intensified when accompanied by fasting, whether fasting from sleep as Jesus did in Luke 6, or something else, most commonly food.

When Lisa and I had arrived in England and settled into our flat, I picked a night to fast from sleep, praying to God for guidance about my dissertation topic. I had never prayed like this before, but I felt that through Ed's sermon the Lord was leading me in this direction. I began praying at 10:00 p.m. During the night, I sang worship songs and read through a good portion of the New Testament, thinking that perhaps God would say something to me through his Word. Mostly, however, I prayed. I prayed everything that I could think of praying. I prayed through my hopes and fears regarding school. I prayed through all the ways that God had guided me up to this point. But I specifically prayed for a dissertation topic, telling God over and over that I was not wise enough to come up with this on my own.

By around 5:30 a.m. I had not heard anything from the Lord. Nothing. I was strongly disappointed. Although I knew better, the whole thing felt like a waste. My eyes heavy with sleep, I picked 6:00 a.m. as the close of my all-night prayer session. I resolved to pray one last time for specific guidance from God and then call it quits. At around 5:55, the most amazing thing happened: a question popped into my head that I had never really thought about before. In many ways it was a fresh question that crystallized much of what I had been thinking about over the past three or four years. Suddenly I was wide awake. God had given me my topic! I can't even begin to describe the excitement of that moment. He actually spoke to me during my prayers![2]

Betty Huizenga, the founder of a ministry called Apples of Gold, describes a similar experience:

> My husband and I had just sold our business and retired. He was feeling exuberant, and I was feeling a loss. . . . I took a long

walk one afternoon. I asked God what he wanted me to do with my life at this time of change. Actually, I was crying out to him from my heart. I wanted my life to have value and I wanted to serve God. I found a chair on the porch of an old cabin and sat down. The Lord began to speak to my mind—not in a still small voice, but with a voice of calling. There have been many times in my life when I have felt especially close to God, but never have I felt this type of call. . . . As I sat there, the Lord clearly and directly laid out the entire idea, program, Scriptures and method for Apples of Gold to me.[3]

Toran and Brenda know what this is like. They were attending church on Father's Day, 2009. At the end of the sermon there was a time of silent reflection in order to listen to God. Each father was to ask God how he could use his gifts to serve in the body of Christ. Toran was already quite active in serving, but he obediently prayed, "God, is there anything that you want me to do to serve you?" And then he listened. Confident God had nothing else for him to do, Toran was caught completely by surprise when in the middle of that silence God impressed upon his heart that he and Brenda were to adopt Max, a special needs baby they knew needed a home. While they were for adoption in theory, they had never even considered the possibility of adopting Max. As Toran describes it, time stood still. He was talking to God for what seemed like forever, even though only a few moments passed. Could they handle another child? They already had three small children at home. What was Brenda going to think of this idea? Why Max? Why a special needs child? Yet at the end of that silent conversation with the Lord, Toran was convinced that they needed to adopt Max. His one request, however, was that God be the one to convince Brenda. A year later, Toran and Brenda welcomed Max into their home as their son.

So how did God convince Brenda? Through an inner prompting of the Holy Spirit, something we will look at right after discussing God's leading through corporate prayer.

Corporate Prayer (and Fasting)

God guides during times of individual prayer. He also guides during times of corporate prayer. Consider what happened in Acts 13 in the church at Antioch. The church had gathered together and, "while they were worshiping the Lord and fasting, the Holy Spirit said, 'Set apart for me Barnabas and Saul for the work to which I have called them'" (Acts 13:2). The combination of worshiping and fasting indicates the church in Antioch was probably having a communal prayer service.[4] One commentator notes that the fact that they were fasting indicates the church was "in a mood of particular expectancy and openness to the Lord's leading."[5] God spoke into the middle of this prayer service to the whole church—perhaps through one of the prophets or through a general conviction given to all during the time of prayer.

Another great Bible example is found in 2 Chronicles. Jehoshaphat, the king of Judah, discovered that a vast enemy army was preparing to attack. "Alarmed, Jehoshaphat resolved to inquire of the LORD, and he proclaimed a fast for all Judah. The people of Judah came together to seek help from the LORD; indeed, they came from every town in Judah to seek him" (20:3–4). In the midst of the prayer Jehoshaphat cries out: "We do not know what to do, but our eyes are on you" (v. 12). While the assembly was listening, the Spirit of the Lord came on a man named Jahaziel, who by the way was not a prophet but simply one of the thousands of Levites.

> [Jahaziel] said: "Listen, King Jehoshaphat and all who live in Judah and Jerusalem! This is what the LORD says to you: 'Do not be afraid or discouraged because of this vast army. For the battle is not yours, but God's. Tomorrow march down against them. They will be climbing up by the Pass of Ziz, and you will find them at the end of the gorge in the Desert of Jeruel. You will not have to fight this battle. Take up your positions; stand firm and see the deliverance the LORD will give you, Judah and Jerusalem. Do not be afraid; do not be discouraged. Go out to face them tomorrow, and the LORD will be with you'" (2 Chron. 20:15–17).

How's that for a specific answer! Israel's prayer for guidance was directly answered during the time of corporate prayer.

We experienced something similar during our search for a worship pastor, a difficult and dangerous task that ranks just below facing an invading enemy horde. The search committee had committed themselves to fasting and praying one day a week, asking for God's guidance. Through this process, one candidate had emerged. Yet the committee could not get any clear direction that this person was exactly whom God had chosen. It was as if heaven had closed and God was no longer providing counsel. Unsure why, someone on the committee suggested that perhaps God was refusing to answer because he wanted the whole congregation to seek him in prayer, so that the whole church would grow in this process. This suggestion resonated with the committee, so they called three communal fasting and prayer sessions for the church, following the examples of Acts 13 and 2 Chronicles 20. At the end of the three sessions, notecards were passed around and everyone who felt they had heard something from the Lord was asked to write it down. When the cards were collected, it was clear that God had been saying the same thing to several individuals independently. The committee rejoiced at God's faithfulness. There was a strong sense that God was telling the church to move forward with this candidate. A month later, he was hired.

The Inner Prompting of the Spirit

Remember the story of Toran and Brenda being told by God to adopt Max? God spoke to Toran during a time of prayer, and he spoke to Brenda while she was reading a novel one day. Although there was nothing special about the novel, while she was reading it an inward compulsion and peace from the Holy Spirit came over her. She knew God wanted her and Toran to adopt Max. There was no rational explanation as to why she felt this peace at that moment. It simply came because the Spirit chose that moment to move in her heart.

Something similar happened one day during the time of the early church, when a man named Philip was told by God to go to the road that runs from Jerusalem to Gaza. There he found a chariot traveling the route. In the chariot was a high-ranking Ethiopian official, reading the book of Isaiah. The Spirit told Philip, "Go to that chariot and stay near it" (Acts 8:29).

Picturing this scene in my mind, I always envisioned God's booming voice thundering from heaven to communicate audibly with Philip. I never stopped to wonder: If God spoke audibly, wouldn't the Ethiopian official have heard it too? The longer I have pondered this story, the more I am convinced that commentator David Peterson is right to describe the Spirit speaking to Philip as "the *inward assurance* that he should approach this high-ranking man."[6] After all, Acts is trying to make the point that God lives within believers.

Charles Spurgeon, referencing this story in Acts, comments,

> There are many monitions [directions] from God's Spirit which are not noticed by Christians when they are in a callous condition; but when the heart is right with God and living in communion with God, we feel a sacred sensitiveness, so that we do not need the Lord to shout, but His faintest whisper is heard. Nay, he need not even whisper . . . in your soul, as distinctly as the Spirit said to Philip, "Go near and join thyself to this chariot," you shall hear the Lord's will. As soon as you see an individual, the thought shall cross your mind, "Go and speak to that person."[7]

I love the varied language Peterson and Spurgeon use: "inward assurance," "directions from God's Spirit," "sacred sensitiveness," "faintest whisper," and a "thought crossing your mind." These give a sense of what we mean by inner promptings of the Holy Spirit. Earlier I told the story of God choosing a wife for me, a process of his guiding that began with the Spirit whispering the idea to me while I was sitting in the class her father was teaching. That is an inner prompting of the Holy Spirit. Modern-day cynics may humorously dismiss such a notion as mistaking indigestion for the Spirit, but the inner prompting of the Spirit is a very common way that God provides guidance and direction.

In one sense, most guidance and counsel from God could be described as the inner promptings of the Holy Spirit, whether it comes through prayer, God's Word, or whatever means. But in another sense, this is something distinct. The inner prompting of the Spirit is an indefinable sense that God is telling you which way to go and what to do, usually at a completely unexpected time.

Casting of Lots

How do you choose between two seemingly equally qualified candidates? After you have gone through the process of narrowing down a broad field of potential replacements for an open position, and two remain, how do you choose between them? This was the dilemma the followers of Jesus faced in Acts 1. They knew they needed a replacement for Judas Iscariot, who had betrayed Jesus. After agreeing on the necessary qualifications and screening all who were present, two equally viable candidates emerged: Justus and Matthias. But only one could fill Judas's spot. How were they to choose? So they prayed, "Lord, you know everyone's heart. Show us which of these two *you have chosen*" (v. 24). Then they cast lots. The lot fell to Matthias, and he was added to the twelve apostles.

Casting lots was a well-known ancient procedure that used seeming "chance" to help make a decision. Most likely the casting of lots involved marking stones and drawing them out of a bag. Today it might be comparable to flipping a coin or drawing straws. Of course, there is no such thing as luck in God's world. Proverbs 16:33 says, "The lot is cast into the lap, but its every decision is from the LORD." Well-known in the Old Testament, casting lots was used in the Bible to allot sections of the Promised Land to the various tribes of Israel (see Josh. 18:6), to divide the priests into groups (see 1 Chron. 24), to determine the order for bringing offerings of wood (see Neh. 10:34), to decide who should live in the rebuilt city of Jerusalem (see Neh. 11:1), and to identify Jonah as the reason for the pagan sailors' troubles on the boat to Tarshish (see Jonah 1:7). Lots may also have been used to select Saul as king of Israel (see 1 Sam. 10:20–21) and identify Achan as the offending party (see Josh. 7).

Although the casting of lots is always presented positively in the Bible, some today dismiss the practice. To them, once the Holy Spirit came at Pentecost there was no more need for the casting of lots.[8] But did the Holy Spirit need the casting of lots in the Old Testament? He was perfectly capable of communicating his leading without it, as in the case of God telling Samuel which of Jesse's sons to anoint king, a passage the apostles are referring to when they pray, "Lord, you know everyone's heart" (see 1 Sam. 16:7). So any theory that the casting of lots was for Old Testament believers and the leading of the Spirit is for New Testament believers should be viewed as highly suspect. More accurately, we should say the Holy Spirit always leads and guides. Sometimes he uses the casting of lots. Sometimes he doesn't.[9]

John Piper urges strong caution in casting lots, but he gives an example of how the church he pastors, Bethlehem Baptist Church, regularly uses this method to determine God's leading. Bethlehem has both staff elders and lay elders. In order to have a valid quorum for their elder meetings they require a certain proportion of those voting to be lay elders. If there are too many staff elders present, they cast lots to determine which staff elders should be allowed to vote.[10]

Many churches (including ours) use casting lots to select their elders and deacons. The March 2008 issue of *Reformed Worship* reported an increase in churches using this method to allow God to select their church leadership. What churches have found is that when they used popular vote to select elders and deacons, only the most popular people were selected—hardly an indication that God was the one doing the selecting.[11] In contrast, those who have been selected through the casting of lots felt that God had selected them for their positions of leadership.

Perhaps the way to heed John Piper's wise caution, while still affirming what Bethlehem Baptist Church (and other churches) do in practice, is to recognize that the casting of lots appears designed more for public, as opposed to private, decisions. That is, decisions a group must make together, as opposed to decisions that an individual makes for him- or herself. Acts 1, Joshua 18, 1 Chronicles 24, and Jonah 1 all describe corporate decisions when a group of people collectively needed guidance from the Lord. A public setting for casting lots might also be inferred from Proverbs 18:18, which says, "Casting the lot settles disputes and keeps strong opponents apart."

When casting lots, it is important to read Acts 1 carefully. Casting lots is not a shortcut to avoid the rigors of actually determining which options are valid. Casting lots is meant to decide between multiple *valid* options, not all *conceivable* options. The apostles cast lots only after they had narrowed down the list to Justus and Matthias. When our church selects elders and deacons using the casting of lots, this comes only after a long selection process designed to identify qualified candidates—the qualifications of which are clearly spelled out in Scripture (see 1 Tim. 3; Titus 1). We cannot simply flout God's commands to identify qualified candidates and expect that he will select the right ones through the casting of lots. Additionally, casting lots is not a shortcut taken to avoid praying. In Acts 1 the disciples were constantly in prayer (see v. 14). And before they cast lots, the apostles specifically prayed for God to communicate through the casting of lots (see v. 24).

One final observation regarding casting lots: casting lots appears aimed at selecting from multiple valid options rather than being used for "yes/no" questions. In other words, the apostles were not seeking an answer to the "yes/no" question, "Have you chosen Matthias to be the twelfth apostle?" They were asking, "Between Justus and Matthias, whom are you choosing to be the twelfth apostle?", an opportunity to select between two valid options. If the apostles had a sense that God had already chosen Matthias and wanted to confirm that, there is another means available for hearing from the Lord. It is called "putting out a fleece."

Putting Out a Fleece

Gideon was the least in his family and was from the smallest clan in Manasseh. He was not the person anyone, including himself, would expect to free Israel from Midianite oppression. So when God showed up to call Gideon to lead Israel, Gideon was understandably confused. More than that, given the magnitude of the task and his lack of confidence in his qualifications, Gideon was terrified. He needed confirmation to convince him he had heard God correctly. Choosing his own sign, he asked God something like: "If you are really telling me to do this job, then let this fleece I am leaving on the ground overnight be wet with dew while the ground remains dry." Miraculously, what Gideon specified happened. Gideon then asked for another sign, just to be sure. "This time," he asked, "let the ground be wet and the fleece dry" (see Judg. 6). Again God did what Gideon asked, thereby confirming his direction.

Because of this passage, the process of asking God for direction or confirmation through these kinds of signs is known as "putting out a fleece." While this way of approaching God draws its name from this passage, there are other places in the Bible where signs are used to identify or confirm God's leading. Abraham's servant asked God to make known which girl he had chosen to be Isaac's wife by having her offer, in specific words, to provide water for the servant's camels without being asked (see Gen. 24:14). When Jonathan wanted to know if God was leading him to attack the Philistines, he too asked for specific wording from the Philistines as a sign from God (see 1 Sam. 14:10).[12]

Francis Schaeffer became a Christian in his teenage years. After his conversion, he became convinced he should not follow the path his father had laid out for him. Instead, God was calling him to go to college and pursue going into ministry. Francis's wife Edith retells the story of the confrontation between Francis and his father one morning.

> When Fran came down in the morning, Pop was standing by the front door. Turning to give Fran a long, hard look, he said, "I don't want a son who is a minister, and—I don't want you to go.". . . Then Fran asked in a strained voice, "Pop, give me a few minutes to go down in the cellar to pray." In a fear of uncertainty as to what to do . . . he went down and wept and wept . . . hot tears of sorrow for his father. He knew there was a choice that must be made in minutes, and he wanted to make it exactly as God would have him make it. But how to know what the will of God was? In an act of desperate and simple faith, he did what he wouldn't advise anyone else to do, but what he felt was the only right thing for him to do then. He prayed (if anyone ever prayed sincerely, he did then), "Oh, *please*, God show me. . . ." Then he took out a coin—"heads I'll go in spite of Dad's desires"—and he tossed it. It was heads. Still weeping, he cried out, "God, be patient with me. If it comes up tails this time . . . I'll go." He flipped it again, and it was tails. A third time he pleaded, "Once more, God . . . I don't want to make a mistake with Dad upstairs. Please now, let it be heads again," and it was heads. So he went upstairs . . . to his dad and said, "Dad, I've *got* to go. . . ." His dad looked hard at him, then went out to slam the door. . . . But just before the door hit the frame, his voice came through, "I'll pay for the first half year." . . . It was many years later that Pop became a Christian, but Fran thinks this moment was the basis of his salvation.[13]

While flipping a coin may sound like casting lots, Francis Schaeffer's story is actually an example of putting out a fleece. Schaeffer is not trying to select between two equally valid options. He is trying to confirm God's leading in the face of stiff opposition from his father. This is what Gideon was doing with his fleece.

Dani Johnson, Christian author, financial adviser, and motivational speaker, tells of her use of a fleece in determining God's leading as to whether she should appear on ABC's *Secret Millionaire*. When first asked, she adamantly refused. "But quickly we found out that we were fighting God and not man," she said.

"It was crazy," she continued. "We said, no, no, no, no, no, and God made it obvious that he had opened up this door. Like Gideon, we laid out a fleece before the Lord—four fleeces, in fact, and asked for the impossible . . . and he did it." When asked what the fleeces were, Dani replied, "Without compromising my relationship with ABC, I shouldn't say. I'll just say they were impossible things that had to come together; there was just no way it was going to work. But every single one of those things worked out. It was God, that's the bottom line."[14]

A few words of wisdom about using fleeces: if we are to follow Gideon's example (and Francis Schaeffer's) then we must first ask God's permission. In Judges 6:39, Gideon said, "Do not be angry with me. Let me make just one more request." Likewise Francis Schaeffer prayed, "Please, God show me" and "God, be patient with me." God decides how he wants to communicate his guidance and so we must ask him for permission to use a fleece. But how do we know if God gives his permission? If the fleece happens. This is why a fleece usually only works to give a "yes" answer. If the fleece comes out "no," it is not clear if God is saying "no" to using the fleece or "no" to the actual question. Along these same lines, a fleece has to be something out of the ordinary that would require God to intervene. If we say, "Lord, if the sun comes up tomorrow then I will take it that you want me to apply for this promotion," we should not assume that we have heard from the Lord! A better fleece might be, "Lord, if this Friday my boss is in his office despite the fact that it is his day off and he brings up the idea of me applying for this promotion, then I will take it that this is from you." Again, if the boss is not in on Friday that doesn't mean God doesn't want you to apply for the promotion; he may be saying that he doesn't want to tell you this way. However, if your boss is in on Friday and does bring up the idea unprompted, I would think that God has spoken to you.

Beware, however, of "fleece-mania." This is the tendency to constantly be thinking of little fleeces all day long for little decisions, such as saying to oneself, *If this file is not on my computer desktop, then I will assume I am not supposed to work on that right now.* This does not seem to be how God designed for these to work.

Sometimes, however, we don't even know what to ask God for, except that we need some sort of sign as to his leading. This was the case for Lewis Sperry Chafer, who in the spring of 1924 was wrestling with overwhelming doubts because of the financial pressures associated with the founding of what would become Dallas Theological Seminary.

> At four o'clock on a never-to-be-forgotten morning, I wakened with a sense of deep foreboding with regard to the agreement reached in Dallas. It seemed as if an unbearable burden had been thrust upon me. Failure, probable if not certain, was the only thing I could see, and all the forebodings the powers of darkness could devise came rolling like billows over me. In a great agony of spirit I cried to God saying I could not go through the day without some definite indication of his will in the matter. If such indication were not given, I should have to cable to Dallas requesting them to discontinue the whole project.[15]

Chafer fell back asleep. Later that morning at breakfast, the person he was staying with began to inquire about the school he was planning. By the end of the day, his host had requested the privilege of purchasing all the books for the library and paying Chafer's yearly salary. Chafer was elated. God had answered his request for a sign and confirmed the direction he had laid upon Chafer's heart.

This, too, is a kind of fleece.

Spiritual Direction from Others

Should someone devote their life solely to prayer and meditation, or should he or she include a ministry of preaching? Okay, so this is not a decision that many of us would lose sleep over today, but in the thirteenth century St. Francis of Assisi found this choice weighing heavily on his shoulders. (It would also have far-reaching consequences for the whole world, through the

Franciscan monks who would follow his example.) Longing for guidance and direction, Francis asked two of his most trusted friends to each independently meet with another spiritually attuned companion and seek the Lord's will in this matter. The two groups of two prayed for guidance from God. Both groups concluded that God was telling Francis he should "go about the world preaching, because God did not call you for yourself alone but also for the salvation of others."[16]

Spiritual direction from others is not simply wise advice. Spiritual direction comes through another's interaction with the Lord on your behalf. St. Francis's friends and their prayer partners, who presumably did not even know Francis, were not telling him what the wise thing to do would be. They were communicating what they had heard the Lord say. This was often the role of the prophet in the Old Testament. In David's life, a prophet such as Nathan played more of the role of spiritual director, while his advisors such as Ahithophel or Hushai provided good advice.

A modern example of spiritual direction happened in the life of an engineer named Jim. Talented and entrepreneurial, Jim was doing quite well at a small start-up company in Ann Arbor. Jim and his wife Judy were also committed to serving the Lord outside of work, including helping put on a crusade in Ann Arbor for Nicky Cruz, a famous evangelist. While driving Nicky back to the airport after the crusade was over, Jim was floored when Nicky said to him, "I think God wants you to come and be my director of operations." Listen to Jim's own words about this experience:

> Judy and I had been praying and preparing financially for vocational Christian service for about three years. I had applied for several positions I felt I was qualified for and there was dead silence, no answers. We had essentially given up hope that God had any plans for us in this direction when Nicky asked the question. We did in fact receive positive feedback from people we respected who we talked with. I remember clearly being in the bedroom on my knees praying for confirmation the night

before I needed to resign my current position and leave many close friendships. I don't subscribe to Bible roulette, however after I had prayed I picked up my Bible, which was open on the bed, and read Matthew 19 and came across this verse: "And everyone who has left houses or brothers or sisters or father or mother or children or lands, for my name's sake, will receive a hundredfold and will inherit eternal life." This gave me the affirmation I needed to move ahead.[17]

One of the problems with spiritual direction is that it is easily abused. One Christian can easily mislead another simply by saying, "God wants you to. . . ." But, as with all these means, their abuse at the hands of immature Christians does not negate God's legitimate use of these methods. A few warnings, however, are in order.

First, consider the source! God is more likely to provide spiritual direction through certain people close to you who have your best interests in mind, people such as your spouse, your grown children, mentors, accountability partners, and close friends. He also is most likely to provide direction through pastors, elders, spiritual leaders, and parents. These people are given responsibility for providing guidance and direction, and God supports that. In all cases, be very leery of direction that comes from immature believers or where there is a conflict of interest (such as with one teenager wanting to date another!). Second, I would ask God for multiple confirmations, just like Francis did. If God is providing spiritual direction, he will surely tell two different people the same thing. If a pastor tells you that God has highlighted your name for a specific ministry, I would look for confirming direction from a spouse or close friend. In the absence of such confirmation, I would be leery.

One final example of spiritual direction: it was January, 2009; I needed to know what book God wanted us to study as a church. Seeking God's guidance through spiritual direction, I asked a group of men I regularly meet with for study and the pastoral staff of the church to seek guidance from God. A few weeks passed. One of the pastors stuck his head in my office. "John," he informed me. "I don't know why, I just think it is supposed to be John." Okay. I made a mental note, but didn't tell anyone. Another month passed. A member of my study group sent me a long email telling me that he just couldn't stop thinking that God wanted us to study the Gospel of John. Weeks went by. I asked the rest of the study group if they had heard anything, never mentioning the two suggestions about John. One said either Luke or John; another said he felt strongly it was supposed to be a Gospel. The others agreed. Their spiritual direction, along with one other piece of communication from God, convinced me John was it.

Circumstances

Weeks before anyone began providing direction about what we were to study next, my father-in-law gave me my eagerly antic- ipated annual Christmas present: a theological book (I know I'm weird). December 2008's present was a theology of the Gospel of John. At the time, the choice seemed random and insignificant. By the end of February 2009, it had dawned on me that the choice was not random, but another message from God that John was indeed the book we were supposed to study.

James Fenhagen once wrote, "Every event, every encounter carries within it the potential for an encounter with God. And as these events pass and are carried in memory, the potential for dialogue remains."[18] Ben Campbell Johnson adds, "Most of us can look back on a number of days that were marked by a chance meeting, a phone call, an accident of circumstance, a penetrating insight, a conversation, or another of a myriad of seemingly small events that today hold special significance for us. . . . When we recognize the influence of these occurrences, it makes us wonder if under the veil of the ordinary God isn't whispering a word in our ears."[19]

One evening, a young couple named Dan and Megan "hap- pened" to be spending time in a group talking about school choices for children. The seemingly innocuous conversation made a deep impression on Dan and Megan as they listened. Something began to stir in Dan that maybe God was telling them they needed to transfer their kids to a public school. As they talked about it together, Dan and Megan decided to get a tour of the public school their children could be attending. After the official tour was over, a woman named Dixie came up to them. She was one of the janitors at the school. "Are you followers of Jesus?" she boldly asked. Hearing their affirmative reply, Dixie continued, "I've worked for twenty-three years as a custodian in the school system. I clean all night and pray all morning for the kids. I sit in the broom closet and ask God to show me a child who needs him, then I pray. As I clean the chairs I pray for the child who will sit there, that God will be present and will send his angels to encamp around the child. I've done it for countless children God has shown me and I'll do it for yours. This is where you are supposed to be."[20] How cool is that! (Can we get Dixie at our kids' school?) This seemingly "random" conversation gave Dan and Megan the peace that this was indeed God's leading and guiding.

Lindsey, a young adult living in the UK, tells a story of God guiding her through circumstances when looking for a job. She says,

I really didn't know what I wanted to do, but prayed that God would guide me. Shortly after that I received a newsletter from a Christian organization which I had been involved with and really respected. On opening the newsletter, the first thing I saw and which really stood out, was a job advert for a bilingual secretary (Spanish and English), in Oxford. I had studied Spanish at university and had spent some time living in Spain, so a job where I could use my Spanish was ideal. I decided to apply and prayed God would close the door on this opportunity if it wasn't right. . . . On the day of the interview I remember being struck by how God is evident even in the small, seemingly unimportant details of life. As I got on the coach to take me from Oxford to Gatwick ready to fly back to Barcelona, I realized that I knew the coach driver who was Spanish. . . . I don't believe that this was a chance encounter, but that through it God was confirming that he was guiding me all the way.[21]

Dreams and Visions

In Acts 16 Paul and his companions had made plans to take the gospel farther into Asia. But one night, while Paul was sleeping, a man from Macedonia appeared to Paul in a dream, asking him to come and share the gospel with them. When Paul awoke he shared that dream with his companions. Interestingly, the text says that Paul and his companions then spent time discussing the dream together. Only after that time of communal discernment did they conclude together that God was guiding them not farther into Asia, but to Europe.

Such dreams were quite common in the beginning of Matthew's Gospel. God communicated direct guidance to Joseph four times by dream (1:20; 2:13, 19, 22) and once to the three wise men (2:12).

But God doesn't communicate that way today, does he? Steve and Cindy probably thought not—until just a few years ago. Steve tells their story:

> God had impressed upon Cindy's heart that we needed to move to a new house. However I didn't warm up to the idea until we were in Central Asia on an eight-week missions trip. While we were there, we fell in love with a large group of missionaries and invited all of them to our house (not sure where they would sleep but we decided that we would figure that out later). Having heard from Cindy about God's prompting, I spent a day fasting about the possibility of moving. Reading through Acts the examples of people using their homes to board the apostles and for worship shined off the pages like a light bulb. It was now clear to me that we needed to look at homes with more room so that Cindy could exercise her gift of hospitality.
>
> When we got home we didn't know God's timeline so we decided to sell our house before we looked seriously at houses. At that time houses were not selling very well, but our house sold in six weeks! So now we needed to find the house that GOD wanted us to have. My prayer for years on many things has been "God I'm a little thick, I want to follow you so please speak loud and clear."
>
> It was during this time that I had the dream (more vivid than your average dream; I can still see it in my mind). In the dream I

saw a light on a garage. In fact the light was probably one of the most common lights that you will ever find on a rural outbuilding. However, after looking at dozens and dozens of houses I NEVER saw this light. However, when our realtor brought us out to visit a house that I had told him we weren't interested in, I saw the light from the dream. I was blown away—and a little confused because I knew Cindy didn't like this house. I discreetly snapped a picture of the light and the garage with my phone and continued with the tour. It was interesting to see everyone warm up to this place. It wasn't until later in the day after we discussed it and I found out that we were all on the same page about this house that I told them about my dream story.[22]

I have not personally experienced God communicating with me through a dream. I have had the experience where I have been lying in bed late at night, thinking and praying through a problem or an issue—and suddenly an answer pops into my head seemingly out of nowhere. This is probably different than having a dream or vision, but the demarcating lines do become a little blurry. I do know that God spoke through dreams and visions in the Bible, and promised that this would continue into this age. As Peter says, God has promised to "pour out my Spirit on all people; your sons and daughters will prophesy; your young men will see visions, your old men will dream dreams" (Acts 2:17).

For this reason, I encourage people not to ignore dreams or visions. Every dream, however, requires careful discernment. St. Francis of Assisi once had a dream from the Lord that he misinterpreted as a call to be a soldier! God appeared to him again in a dream to tell him he had not discerned correctly and later sent a leper across his path to help Francis realize God was calling him to serve in *God's* army as a minister of the gospel, especially to the poor.[23]

Passions and Peace

Guidance is as much about our hearts as it is about our heads. We make decisions not simply because we are rationally convinced, but because we often feel this is the right thing to do. It is not surprising then that God, who created us this way, often communicates with us through our emotions, specifically through our passions and what we might call *peace*.

First, our passions. Psalm 37:4 says, "Take delight in the LORD, and he will give you the desires of your heart." The key to understanding the verse is the opening phrase, "Take delight in the LORD." Once that has happened, the desires of one's heart can be a way in which God communicates guidance regarding which way to go in life.

For example, someone who has committed to serving God overseas may find that God begins to create in his or her heart a passion for a particular people group. David Platt tells the true story of a family in the church where he ministers. Craig, Amy, and their three children had a desire to sell their home and move to another part of the world in order to serve God. David relates more details of their story:

> On top of all this, they had been dealing with various health problems that Amy was experiencing. This was threatening to limit their ability to go overseas because Amy's health might require her to live in a particular climate that would be more conducive to her health. With tears in their eyes, Craig and Amy shared how God had led their hearts to one particular country. When they went to her doctor to ask his opinion on how Amy would fare in that climate, the doctor said that she would actually do better in that climate than in the United States.[24]

The phrase "God had led their hearts to one particular country" is another way of saying that God can use desires of our hearts to guide us.

Warning: this is one of the ways of hearing from God that is most easily abused. One of the biggest obstacles to hearing from God is the fact that our minds and hearts are filled with our own desires, some of which may not be from God. Furthermore, it is even possible that a "godly" desire is not from God. David, author of Psalm 37:4, at one time had a strong and "godly" desire to build God a house. When he communicated this to Nathan the prophet, Nathan replied, "Whatever you have in mind, go ahead and do it, for the LORD is with you" (2 Sam. 7:3). In other words: "David, you have delighted yourself in the Lord, so follow the desires of your heart." However, in this case there were extenuating circumstances that neither Nathan nor David could have understood, so God stepped in and said, "No, this is for your son to build."

God also speaks through a sense of peace, or a lack thereof. This is best illustrated by an event from the life of the apostle Paul.

Paul had just arrived in Troas. His gospel ministry was flourishing. He had everything that he needed: a small Christian community, a home base from which to operate, and lots of receptivity to the gospel. Troas was an "open door." But as he worked there, an unsettled feeling kept gnawing away at him. Titus was supposed to meet him there, but he hadn't come. Was it because things had gone astray in Corinth? Paul was desperately worried that Satan was tearing apart this strategic church that he dearly loved. He had sent Titus there with a strongly worded letter. What if it was poorly received? This nagging feeling that something was wrong kept eating away at Paul. Yes, there was an open door in Troas, but if this was from the Lord why was he so unsettled in his spirit? So in Paul's words, "Now when I went to Troas to preach the gospel of Christ and found that the Lord had opened a door for me, I still had *no peace of mind*, because I did not find my brother Titus there. So I said goodbye and went on to Macedonia" (2 Cor. 2:12–13).

We know this story because the Corinthian church accused Paul of being fickle in his decisions and making his plans using human thinking alone. Paul was writing to tell them that, no, it was the Spirit who was guiding him in his travel plans (see 2 Cor. 1:15–22). One of the means the Spirit used was a lack of peace, motivated by Paul's deep concern and love for the Corinthians.

The converse can also be a way in which God speaks to our hearts; that is, a sense of supernatural peace that passes understanding when we are walking down the path on which God is guiding us.

Human Wisdom and Advice

The final way I want to share in which God can talk with us is the one most easily misunderstood and most easily overemphasized for many. I have entitled it "human wisdom and advice" to differentiate it from the "wisdom from God" mentioned in James 1:5 and 3:17. Wisdom from God refers to any guidance and direction that come directly from God. It can be communicated to us through the Bible, prayer, circumstances, or any of the ways mentioned in this chapter. Human wisdom, on the other hand, is the wisdom accumulated through life experience, education, or carefully pondering the seeming truisms of life. The point here is that God does use human wisdom at times to guide and direct us.

For instance, one day I was sitting in a friend's study, thinking and praying about vision, staffing, and the culture of our church. Feeling lost, I glanced at his library and the first book that caught my eye was *Good to Great* by Jim Collins. Having heard positive things about it, I had always meant to read it. On this day, I felt compelled to stop what I was doing and read the book. I read it cover to cover, and as I did, I felt as though God were opening my mind and answering some of my questions through the human wisdom I was reading.

Or consider the divorced mother who has been praying desperately for God to help her figure out what to do with a troubled child. She visits a counselor who suggests, based on her human experience, that there might be unresolved issues from the divorce. In this human wisdom the mother hears the voice of God counseling her on what to do.

Proverbs 11:14 says, "For lack of guidance a nation fails, but victory is won through many advisers" and Proverbs 24:6 says, "Surely you need guidance to wage war, and victory is won through many advisers." Moses received good advice from his father-in-law Jethro about delegating to others (see Exod. 18). An important story from the life of David affirms the same point.

One day when David was running from Saul, waiting for God to make him king, he sent a request to a man named Nabal. It was sheep-shearing time—a festive time in Israel. David and his men had provided free protection for Nabal's servants and their sheep. Although Nabal had not asked for this favor, it was quite a generous one. On that festive day David decided to request from Nabal whatever food he could spare. Nabal foolishly refused. Raging with anger, David set out to kill Nabal and his household.

When Abigail, Nabal's wife, heard what he had done, she raced out to meet David, bringing him lavish gifts of food. Abigail begged David to ignore Nabal's foolishness. She then advised David that, although he was right to be offended, killing Nabal would be a stain upon his hands. She reminded David that God was with him and had mighty things prepared for him; Nabal wasn't worth him soiling his sword over.

When David heard Abigail's wise advice, he recognized it as guidance provided by God. He said to her, "Praise be to the LORD, the God of Israel, who sent you today to meet me. May you be blessed for *your good judgment* and for keeping me from bloodshed this day and from avenging myself with my own hands" (1 Sam. 25:32–33, emphasis mine). Although David had not asked for it, Abigail's "good judgment" was a means that God used to guide David.

However, although God speaks through godly counsel, not all counsel is from the Lord, even when it comes from genuine Christian believers. The problem with human wisdom is that it cannot be relied upon. Human wisdom can also lead you astray when God is not speaking through it. And not only does God not often speak through human wisdom, Job 12:20 says, "He silences the lips of trusted advisers and takes away the discernment of elders." God often guides us to do things that are completely against human wisdom. After all, no one would ever sell their possessions and give the money to the poor if human wisdom was their only guiding force! But human wisdom is a means by which God can guide and direct our lives.

Conclusion

Here, then, are twelve ways through which God has provided guidance and direction in the past: the Bible, preaching, prayer, the inner prompting of the Spirit, casting lots, putting out a fleece, godly counsel, spiritual direction, circumstances, dreams and visions, passions and peace, and human wisdom. We can be confident he will continue to provide guidance and direction in the future. Yet, having looked at all these ways God can and does speak, there is still the danger that some of what we hear through these means is not from God. So how do we differentiate between when God is speaking through these means and when it is someone (or something) else?

Discussion Questions

1. Review the twelve ways God communicates with his children. Which of these ways has God used to communicate with you? How did God make his guidance known to you?

2. Were any of these ways new concepts for you on how God might speak to you today? How might you be able to use these means in a decision for which you currently need guidance from God?

3. Which story in this chapter was most compelling to you? Why?

4

how do we distinguish God's voice?

Man tells cops God told him to stroll in the nude," the Associated Press reported on May 20, 2010. "A man who told police that God told him to walk the streets naked to save his soul has been arrested. Thibodaux police responded to an obscenity complaint around 2 a.m. Thursday and found Shafiq Mohamed walking nude down the street. Mohamed was taken into custody and charged with obscenity."

Did God really tell this man to take a stroll in the nude? We are all familiar with stories like this one, where someone makes a dubious claim that "God told me . . ." But what separates Shafiq's story from the others in this book—which to the best of my knowledge represent genuine communications from God? Or what distinguishes Shafiq's story from Isaiah 20, where God does tell Isaiah to walk around at least partly naked?

Consider a biblical example that highlights the problem of distinguishing God's voice. In 1 Samuel 3, the boy Samuel is lying in his bed when he hears a voice calling his name. Immediately Samuel jumps up and rushes to Eli, his mentor.

"Here I am," he said. "You called me."

Eli is befuddled. "I didn't call you, Samuel. Go back and lie down."

Once again in bed, Samuel hears the same voice calling him. Again he thinks it is Eli. Again Eli insists it is not. This scene repeats itself once more, but now Eli awakens to what is happening. "It is not me that is calling you, Samuel. It is the Lord" (see vv. 1–9).

How did Eli recognize that the Lord was calling Samuel, when Samuel didn't? Samuel was unable to distinguish the voice of the Lord from the voice of Eli. Here we have the same problem, albeit expressed differently: How do we recognize the voice of the Lord? When we experience an inner prompting, how can we know whether that inner prompting came from God or somewhere else? When we are given a word of advice, how can we determine if this advice is from the Lord?

Let's begin by first establishing the presupposition that God does indeed have a distinguishable "voice," which he intends for us to be able to recognize, and then we will proceed to discuss how we go about learning to pick out his voice amidst the cacophony of noise in our lives.

Hearing God's Voice

In the story of Samuel and Eli, Eli clearly recognizes the Lord's voice, whereas Samuel does not. The Bible tells us this is because "Samuel did not yet know the LORD. The word of the LORD had not yet been revealed to him" (1 Sam. 3:7). The problem was not that *no one* could recognize God's voice. The problem was that it had not yet been revealed to Samuel as it had to Eli. What is implied in 1 Samuel 3—that God's guiding voice is recognizable—is made explicit in a very important passage in the New Testament, John 10.

In John 10, Jesus calls himself the Good Shepherd. In verses 3–4 he says, "The gatekeeper opens the gate for him, and the sheep *listen to his voice*. He calls his own sheep by name and leads them out. When he has brought out all his own, he goes on ahead of them, and his sheep follow him *because they know his voice*" (emphasis mine).

A shepherd has many responsibilities, including searching for the lost, protecting the vulnerable, and caring for the injured. But a shepherd's most common tasks are leading, guiding, and directing his sheep.

This shepherd metaphor that Jesus applies to himself becomes even richer when we understand that in first-century Near Eastern culture shepherds did not drive their sheep using sheepdogs like in the West; instead they led their sheep by using their voices to call them on.[1] Henry Morton describes seeing this happen one day in Israel:

> Early one morning I saw an extraordinary sight not far from Bethlehem. Two shepherds had evidently spent the night with their flocks in a cave. The sheep were all mixed together and the time had come for the shepherds to go in different directions. One of the shepherds stood some distance from the sheep and began to call. First one, then another, then four or five animals ran towards him; and so on until he had counted his whole flock.[2]

The sheep were trained to hear and recognize the voice of their shepherd. They would respond only to that voice. That is the point Jesus is making here: he has a distinguishable, recognizable voice that his sheep know.

Neuropsychologists such as Daniel Levitin tell us

> people can recognize hundreds, if not thousands, of voices. You can probably recognize the sound of your mother's voice within one word, even if she doesn't identify herself. You can tell your spouse's voice right away, and whether he or she has a cold or is angry with you. Then there are well-known voices—dozens, if not hundreds, that most people can readily identify: Woody Allen, Richard Nixon, Drew Barrymore, W. C. Fields, Groucho Marx, Katharine Hepburn, Clint Eastwood, Steve Martin.[3]

Jesus is saying that he too has a recognizable voice, so we should be able to distinguish guidance that comes from him. But how do we recognize that voice? While Jesus does have a literal voice that is distinguishable from all other audible voice patterns, that isn't what he's talking about. After all, Psalm 19 says, "The heavens declare the glory of God, the skies proclaim the work of his hands. . . . Their voice goes out into all the earth" (vv. 1, 4). In that passage we don't think the word *voice* is literal. *Voice* in Psalm 19 represents the way God communicates through nature to all people. When Jesus says that we can recognize his voice, we understand him to mean that we can identify communication that comes from him.

In *The Two Towers*, the second film in the Lord of the Rings trilogy, there is a point where the wizard Gandalf is confronting Théoden, king of Rohan, in an effort to get him to join the war effort to protect Middle Earth. During their conversation Gandalf (and the audience) hears the audible voice of Théoden, but it is clear that the content of what he is saying is coming from somewhere else. Others may be confused, but Gandalf recognizes the "voice" of the evil Saruman speaking in and through Théoden's audible voice.

Likewise, Ray, a friend of mine, got into his car one day and turned on a Christian radio station that was in the middle of broadcasting a sermon. Although the voice on the radio sounded familiar, Ray couldn't quite place who it was. However, as he listened to the man explain the topic at hand, he recognized the arguments and approach as that of a Christian theologian whose books he had read many times. When the man's name was mentioned at the end of the program, it only confirmed what Ray was already certain of.

In both of these examples, the communication content and patterns were what was recognizable, not the audible vocal qualities. So it is with Jesus's voice. There are certain kinds of things that Jesus says, and certain ways in which he says them. Listen to how Richard Stearns puts it as he recalls a phone call he received as CEO of Lennox Corporation, asking him to consider quitting his job to lead World Vision:

So when I answered that phone call from World Vision in January 1998, I knew that God was on the other end of the line. It was His voice I heard, not the recruiter's: "Rich, do you remember the idealistic young man in 1974 who was so passionate about starving children that he would not even fill out a wedding registry? Take a good look at yourself now. Do you see what you have become? But, Rich, if you still care about those children, I have a job I want you to do."[4]

How did Rich recognize Jesus's voice even though what he was physically hearing was the recruiter's voice? How do we go about learning to recognize the voice patterns of Jesus?

Voice Recognition

Our family recently purchased Rosetta Stone software to help us learn a foreign language. The software is named after the world-famous Rosetta Stone, one of the eighteenth century's most monumental archaeological finds. Until its discovery, no one was able to correctly read ancient Egyptian hieroglyphs; such knowledge had been lost millennia ago, and along with it aspects of ancient Egyptian history. The Rosetta Stone unlocked this unknown language because it contains the same message written in both Egyptian (hieroglyphs and Demotic) and Greek. Using their knowledge of Greek, a known language, scholars were able to unlock the mysteries of Egyptian hieroglyphics, an unknown language.

The Rosetta Stone software employs this principle of using the known to decipher the unknown, not only to teach foreign languages, but also in its voice recognition software. Each time you begin the program, the user is asked to put on a headset and count aloud to five. This trains the software to recognize the user's voice, known in voice recognition terms as "enrollment." Because the software is expecting to hear the numbers one through five in English, it extracts speech patterns from this "known" information and forms a model against which

99

all future "unknown" utterances can be compared. This is how most voice recognition software works.

The key to recognizing Jesus's distinctive voice is to train our minds using his known patterns of communication. And where do we find known patterns of communication from God? There are two places: one essential, the other less so.

The Bible

Simply put: the more immersed in the Bible you are, the easier God's voice of guidance is to recognize. Guaranteed.

The Bible is the Rosetta Stone of God. It is voice recognition enrollment. It is the "known" communication from God that trains us to recognize future "unknown" communication from God. Samuel was unable to recognize the voice of the Lord because he had not yet received the Word of the Lord. The Bible is the Word of the Lord in written form, given to us by God in part to help us recognize Jesus's voice in our lives.

When we read, memorize, meditate, and immerse ourselves in God's Word we learn how he speaks—the kinds of things he says, and the ways he acts and interacts with us. For example, when we hear that God guided Jesus to choose Judas Iscariot as a disciple, we learn that sometimes God tells us to do things that will turn out to be a "failure." Or when we hear God say, "Honor your father and mother," our mind is trained to recognize that the voice in our heads saying, *Call your mom and thank her for all she's done for you,* is probably the Lord's voice of guidance. When the words of Scripture are in our minds, the voice of God is ringing in our ears.

Through immersion in the Word of God we also learn the kinds of people God normally speaks to, when he often speaks to them, and exceptions to these patterns. For example, even a cursory reading of the Bible reveals that God often speaks to people through those he has put in leadership positions over them, which reminds us to look for God's voice in the advice of pastors or parents. Likewise, when the Bible tells us that God spoke through Caiaphas, a non-believer, it opens our minds to understand that God does at times speak through non-believers (see John 11:49–51).

The Bible not only trains us to recognize the voice of the Lord, it is the Word of the Lord—superseding, norming, and judging all other interaction we may claim to have from God. It is impossible for God to lie (see Heb. 6:18) and he is not like us that he should change his mind (see Num. 23:19). We may believe that God has told us to marry a non-Christian, but we have not heard the voice of God correctly because God has told us in his Word that we are not to marry someone who is not a believer in Jesus (see 2 Cor. 6:14). We may believe that God is telling us to pay unfair wages to boost profits, but the Word of God tells us that God would never say such a thing (see James 5:4).[5]

Understanding this principle rescued Nehemiah from a terrible situation. One day Nehemiah received a message from the prophet Shemaiah: "Come see me in private. God has given me a message for you." When Nehemiah arrived, Shemaiah closed the door and said, "God told me that there is a plot to assassinate you. He says you are to flee to the temple and seek asylum inside!" But Nehemiah realized that this was not God's voice speaking to him. How? Because it would have been a sin for him to go inside the temple as Shemaiah was telling him to do (see Neh. 6).

When God wanted ancient Israel to evaluate the guidance they had received and determine whether or not it was valid—whether or not it was from him—he told them to evaluate it against the law they had already been given (see Isa. 8:20). The Bible not only trains us to recognize the voice of God, it definitively rules out certain thoughts and ideas as not from the Lord. For these reasons, the Bible is absolutely essential in the process of learning to recognize the voice of the Lord.

Testimony and Experience

Others' experiences of God, as well as our own, are another important though less vital way through which we learn to recognize the voice of Jesus.

God has not stopped speaking, even though he is no longer providing authoritative revelation like we find in the Bible.[6] All Christians recognize that God is still active in history, using the same voice he uses in Scripture (after all, he has only one voice). As we learn about God's activity in the lives of others, and as we grow in our understanding of his activity in our lives, we become more adept at recognizing his voice. The many stories in this book are not simply illustrative, but hopefully formative, demonstrating how the patterns of God's guidance have looked for specific people in specific situations. Each story should help you better recognize God's voice.

Paul pushes us in this direction in Ephesians 3:14–19, praying that Christians "being rooted and established in love, may have power, together with all the Lord's holy people, to grasp how wide and long and high and deep is the love of Christ" (vv. 17–18). By emphasizing "together," Paul is pointing to the power of communal testimonies. When Christians share how God has guided and directed them, our community of faith grows in our understanding of who God is and how he interacts with his children. The more this happens, the more we are filled with the fullness of God.

So read a biography of a person like Hudson Taylor, and see how God guided him. Listen more closely the next time someone shares a testimony in church about feeling called to adopt, and ask them questions about how that calling came and what it looked like.

Spending time in the Scriptures is most important, but there is something beneficial in the stories of others for learning to recognize God's voice.

Principles for Identifying God's Voice

These six general principles, culled from both the Scriptures and the testimony of believers, have been helpful for me in distinguishing God's voice. These are by no means exhaustive, but I consider them a jumpstart in learning to recognize God's voice.

God Calls Us to Trust Him More

It is helpful to recognize that God usually encourages us down paths that require us to rely more on him and less on ourselves or others. In other words, God usually calls us to adventures that are scarier and more dangerous, and consequently will stretch our faith. Our voice, and the voices of our friends, family, and society, usually encourage us to choose smaller, safer, more manageable, and known things—choices that do not require much faith. As a result, God's guidance often defies human wisdom. To put it bluntly, if we follow God's leading someone should think we are crazy.

In Matthew 10:16, Jesus says, "I am sending you out like sheep among wolves." David Platt, in his book *Radical*, comments:

> Jesus was saying to his disciples then—and, by implication, to you and me now—"I am sending you to dangerous places, where you will find yourself in the middle of evil, vicious people. And you will be there by my design." Jesus told them, "Go to great danger, and let it be said of you what people would say of sheep wandering into the middle of wolves. 'They're crazy! They're clueless! They have no idea what kind of danger they are getting into!' This is what it means to be my disciple." We don't think like this. . . . We think, if it's dangerous, God must not be in it. If it's risky, if it's unsafe, if it's costly, it must not be God's will. But what if these factors are actually the criteria by which we determine something is God's will? What if we begin to look at the design of God as the most dangerous option before us? What if the center of God's will is in reality the most unsafe place for us to be?[7]

Judges 7 is a classic example of this. God has chosen Gideon to lead the Israelites against Midian. After Gideon gathers the men for battle, God makes this ludicrous statement to him: "You have too many men." So God whittles the army down from 32,000 to 300. God then proceeds to lead Gideon and his three-hundred-man army to victory.

Going to battle with 32,000 would have been the safer, wiser strategy. Going to battle with three hundred was the more dangerous, scarier, crazier strategy. But God wanted the Israelites to learn to trust in him, not simply defeat an enemy.

A group of missionaries in the Netherlands' East Indies at the outbreak of World War II could attest to this characteristic feature of God's communication. The group was faced with a choice: leave the island and return home, or stay. Darlene Deibler Rose, one of these missionaries, recorded what happened:

> As we gathered for prayer, Dr. Jaffray [the missionary leader] said, "I want to counsel you not to discuss this decision that must be made with each other—not even husband and wife. Go to your knees and say, 'Lord, what do you want me to do? Shall I go or shall I stay?' This is extremely vital, because then no matter what happens in the months or possibly the years that lie ahead, you will know that you are exactly where God wants you to be. If He leads you to leave, you'll never feel that you were a coward and fled. If you are led to stay, no matter what happens you can look up and say, 'Lord, you intended for me to be right here.'" We earnestly sought guidance. When the truck arrived on Friday, there was not a person among us who felt led to leave. As Dr. Jaffray had said, "God does not work in confusion, a wife against a husband or vice versa, in a matter that concerns both of you. This is but a confirmation to your hearts of His directive."[8]

The seemingly safer and wiser option was to return home. The option that required the most faith was to stay on the island. As with Gideon, they heard God's voice telling them to choose the more dangerous route. Confirmation of this came when the ship they would have been on, had they chosen to leave, was torpedoed three days later, with no known survivors.

While the missionaries did avoid the sinking of the ship, many would end up losing their lives over the next few years in POW camps. However, each one could say that, despite the horrors they endured, this was the journey God had for them. Darlene's comments on her experience are fitting: "It is imperative that we know the voice of the Shepherd and learn to follow Him when He speaks."[9]

My wife Lisa and I have experienced this as well. I can still remember the day the specialist, looking at our baby's ultrasound, sat us down and said, "Not everything is all right here." Staring into our stunned eyes, he proceeded to explain that our child had a potentially very severe health issue that was developing *in utero*. To make matters worse, in two days we were leaving America to return to England where we resided, and we did not understand their foreign (to us) medical system. The specialist wrote up a description of the problem, and told us to give it to the doctors there. For the next three or four months, the situation continued to worsen, until it was decided that labor should be induced early. After our son's birth, we were faced with an agonizing quandary. Our child's condition was such that he was quickly moved to the best hospital in the land. But we kept being told by American doctors watching from afar that the care we were receiving was not what they would recommend. They urged more and different action. Sensing our despair, good friends generously offered to move us back to America and pay our medical expenses for the best treatment available in America (and presumably the world).

But what was God telling us to do? Was he speaking in and through the circumstances of our friends' generosity, telling us to move home? Or was he telling us to stay, having clearly called us to England? To go home was the wiser, safer, more known option. To stay was the scary, dangerous, and unknown option. Never had we faced a more frightening decision. It was one thing to trust God with our own lives, but this choice affected our little boy—and he had no say in it! As we prayed desperately for guidance, I felt as if God was asking me where my trust was: Was it in him or in the American medical system? He reminded me of the story of Abraham being asked to sacrifice Isaac, and how God himself had provided when there seemed to be no other way. Though it was a gut-wrenching decision, we decided God was leading us to stay.

Six years later, when we were living back in America again, the pediatric specialist we had been seeing every six months since returning home gave us the most startling news. When we first went to see him, he had told us (not surprisingly) that he disagreed with the treatment plan followed by our foreign doctors. On this day, however, he walked into the office and informed us that the consensus of the global medical community regarding our child's problem was now shifting away from the American consensus and toward the treatment our child had received overseas!

The reason God often leads us down scarier, dangerous, "unwise" paths is that we grow in our faith when we travel these roads. David Brenner helpfully reminds us, "God's interest in what we do grows out of a much more fundamental interest in who we are."[10] This means that God will usually counsel us toward the option that requires us to trust and rely on him more.

Of course, this doesn't mean that God never guides us to seek the best medical care for a child, or attempt to escape danger, or take the largest army possible into a war. What it means is that *if* we hear a voice urging us to take the road less traveled, the more dangerous and unknown road, the road that requires the most faith, we should pay attention. There is a good chance this is from the Lord.

God Tells Us to Humbly and Sacrificially Love Others

God is love. God's voice is a loving voice. By this I don't mean "warm and cuddly," but rather oriented toward what is most loving. After all, everything God ever commanded anyone to do can be summarized by the commands to love him and others (see Mark 12:29–31; Rom 13:10; Gal. 5:14). Therefore, any advice we hear that is consistent with the law of love is guaranteed to be from the Lord.[11]

Love is a tricky concept, easily perverted, so God anchors the definition of love in the cross of Christ. With the crucifixion of Jesus, God demonstrated what true love looks like: it is not all about warm, fuzzy feelings, but concrete, sacrificial service done in humility, even for one's enemy.

An example of this kind of cross-shaped love comes from John 3. John the Baptist's popularity was waning, while Jesus's was rising. John's disciples inform him of this, expecting that John would do something to reverse this trend. Instead John says to his disciples, regarding Jesus: "He must become greater; I must become less" (v. 30). This humble, sacrificial statement is exactly the kind of thing God tells us.

On November 10, Doris wrote me a note that began, "For over five years I have been crying out to God to help me understand why my husband of over 45 years has Alzheimer's. I've confessed my sins; I've cried; I've prayed; I've fasted—but no answer." As I continued reading, I learned Doris was writing to tell me that on November 7 she had received an answer at last, from the story of John the Baptist. She heard God telling her that she was loving God by choosing to accept this very difficult assignment, just as John had accepted his assignment. When she shared her story with me, it sounded very much like what God would say. It took great humility, and evidenced sacrificial love for both God and her husband, for Doris to accept this assignment, and the voice urging her to do so certainly sounds like God's.

Likewise, James Dobson tells the story of how, at a troubled time in his life, his mother requested help from his dad, a traveling evangelist. Immediately, James's dad cancelled all his speaking engagements and took a less prominent ministry job that involved no traveling so he could be around for his son.[12] That sounds like the kind of humble, sacrificial act of love God would guide someone to do.

God Supports His Social Structures

God has created certain social structures such as marriage, family, government, and church. He does not approve of everything humans do in and through these social structures, but he does support the structures themselves. Therefore, one of the distinguishing characteristics of God's voice is that he directs us in ways that strengthen the social structures he has ordained. God's guidance also supports the leaders he has placed in these structures.

We see this pattern first in the Scriptures. In Galatians 2:1–2, Paul reports he was guided by God through a "revelation" to go to Jerusalem to see the leaders of the church there. While there was nothing these leaders could add to Paul's gospel, it was necessary that Paul's missionary activity be under the authority God had given to the church in Jerusalem, and not undermine it. God did not want a rival power center set up in the Gentile world, so he sent Paul to Jerusalem. This same principle underlies the events of Acts 8, when the Holy Spirit was withheld from the Christians in Samaria until the apostles from Jerusalem came to lay their hands on them. God was supporting the social structure of authority he had given the Twelve and the Jerusalem church. Similarly, in Numbers 16 when Korah, Dathan, and Abiram claim that their rebellion somehow has God's blessing, God shows up immediately to invalidate that claim.

There are many examples of God providing counsel to support the structures he has set up in present-day situations as well. Consider the case of Scott and Dianne, who as newlyweds in the mid-1990s were trying to determine God's leading. Scott had recently received a great job offer from a company in Michigan, whereas Dianne had been accepted to a prestigious nursing program in Chicago. Both opportunities looked as if they could be from the Lord. Which one was truly from God? Scott recalled the situation this way:

> Over and over, in prayer, and fasting, the passage Ephesians 5:25 kept coming to mind ("husbands love your wives as Christ loved the church and *gave himself* for her"). Every time I prayed this passage came to mind, so I began asking God what it looks like to love my wife as Christ does the church? How does this passage apply in this situation? Over time, in prayer, I felt God telling me, "you need to give up your opportunity for her. Sacrifice for her. It is the best way you could start off your marriage." So we moved to Chicago in faith—no job, no friends, no church, nothing. We enrolled her, signed up for the tuition bill, signed a lease, etc., and prayed. A lot. And God provided.[13]

108

Hearing Scott say he sensed God was telling him to put his wife's interests first sounded exactly like the kind of thing God says to husbands. There are, of course, situations where God may guide a couple to do something that is in the husband's best interests, but God designed marriage to be a dance of mutual self-sacrifice in which the husband leads, just as Christ first loved the church and then asked the church to sacrifice in return. Having a husband begin a marriage by putting his wife's interests first is the kind of thing that builds a strong foundation for marriage—and therefore the kind of thing God would have told Scott to do.

On the other hand, Pastor Ed Dobson tells the story of how one Sunday morning a man came up to him and announced, "God told me that I should preach today instead of you!" Wisely, Ed responded, "If that were the case, wouldn't God have told me that as well?" Ed was right to doubt that this was from the Lord, because communicating in this way would subvert the authority structures that God himself had put into place.

Because God supports the social structures he has ordained, it is quite normal to find him speaking to children through their parents, to churches through their elders and pastors, to employees through their bosses, and so on. It also means that God will not tell a husband one thing and a wife another. If such a situation arises, then God's counsel has not yet adequately been discerned.[14]

"God Does Not Work in Confusion"

In trying to learn to distinguish God's voice, it can be helpful to also understand what God's voice does not sound like. As was mentioned in one of the above examples, "God does not work in confusion." Nor does he work in dissension, miscommunication, misunderstanding, disloyalty, or doubt.[15]

For example, two weeks before his wedding, a friend of mine began to experience irrational feelings of doubt and fear of commitment regarding his upcoming marriage. About that time he happened to run into an old girlfriend, who intimated that she missed him. He began to wonder if this was the Lord telling him not to get married. When he asked me, I told him that I didn't think God guided through doubts and fears—or by bringing old girlfriends around two weeks before the wedding. Since my friend had been seeking the Lord's leading during the process of engagement, if God wanted to tell him not to get married he would have done so then, but not through fear of commitment (see below), and definitely not through the temptation to be emotionally unfaithful! Another spiritual mentor for my friend confirmed the same thing.

Or consider the case of a boss who is trying to decide which of two employees to recommend for a promotion. To help her make her decision, this boss discreetly begins to ask around the office for feedback on the two employees. Unbeknownst to her, there is jealousy simmering within her team and a number of her department members conspire to slander the first candidate. On the basis of their lies, the boss recommends the second candidate for the promotion. Was this from the Lord? I don't think so. Lies are Satan's native language (see John 8:44); God cannot lie and doesn't speak through lies. While God does use the evil in this world to accomplish his purposes, when lies are being spoken his voice is not being heard.

Similarly, when a church board genuinely seeking the Lord's leading ends up split in their decision, they should not think they have heard from the Lord. Confusion is not the Lord's way. This does not mean that the process of hearing from God is not sometimes confusing. It means God does not use confusion—or disloyalty, or deceit—to speak words of guidance to us.

God Tells Us Not to Fear

Not only does God not use confusion, he doesn't use fear or discouragement to guide us, either. I am not speaking about fear of God's discipline, which the Holy Spirit does use to keep us away from sinful actions. I am speaking of that panic that can arise as we think about the daunting nature of a task; that fear of failure, or the thought that we are not good enough. Something or someone is trying to discourage us from embracing this path, but it is not God.

When Joshua became discouraged, should he have concluded that God was telling him plans had changed and they were not going to the Promised Land? No. God is the one who commanded him, "do not be afraid; do not be discouraged" (Josh. 1:9).

When Paul began to experience fear because of persecution in Corinth, should he have concluded God was guiding him to leave the city? No. God's was the voice that appeared to him in a vision, saying, "do not be afraid" (Acts 18:9).

Likewise, Darla had been invited by some leaders at her church to accompany a group on a tour of Israel. Having prayed about the decision, Darla felt at the time she was asked that God was encouraging her to go. However, two months before the trip, a recurring illness flared up again. But this time all the various treatments, tests, and medications were not helping her. The illness would not have prevented Darla from going, but if it flared up in Israel she would need the assistance of others. So she was left with a choice: "Am I not getting better from this illness because God does not want me to go to Israel? Or is he asking me to trust him to take care of me even if I get sick there?"

Darla was confused, and was having a hard time praying about the trip. For the first time in her life she felt led to reach out to the church, so she contacted Lisa and Susie, two leaders from a women's group she was part of. When she sat down to meet with them, Darla was stunned and taken aback by the question Susie asked her: "What are you afraid of?" Initially thinking she was not afraid, only confused, Darla felt the Lord open her heart in that moment and allow what she was really feeling to come out: she was afraid of letting people down and of being in a position where she would need others to help her. To this, Lisa calmly responded, "Perfect love casts out fear, so if that is your reason why you think God would not want you to go to Israel, then it is probably not from God."

That was it! Like a ray of sunshine on a cloudy day, God spoke through those words, reassuring Darla that he did want her to go. Her fears melted away. She went on the trip and experienced God's blessings in and through her obedience.

There are many ways that God could have told Darla not to go on the trip. He might have used a lack of finances, a conflicting work schedule, a lack of peace about going, another ministry opportunity, or even a different kind of illness that would have prevented her from going to communicate to Darla that this trip was not for her at this time. The fear of letting people down, however, was not from God.

God Says Unexpected and Mysterious Things

Angela was at the end of her rope. She was in the car on a business trip in San Antonio, Texas, and she was taking stock of her life. She was five months pregnant and often on the road for her company. Upon her leaving for this trip one of her two young children, who was sick, begged her not to go. Angela felt horrible leaving. Her job was incredibly demanding. Her marriage was stressed. And she felt as if she was missing too much of her children's formative years.

> I was crying in the car on the way to the airport to fly home, after a three-day meeting. I knew I needed to stop the career and be home and available to the children. But I was the primary support for our family. My husband's business was still "up and coming" at the time, and wasn't fully able to support us. This is when God told me that he would take care of me and my family. After all, he reminded me, he had always taken care of me, and he reassured me that I could trust him. He wanted me to the stop the career, too. When I arrived at the airport, before boarding my plane to return home, I called my HR person and told them I needed a part-time position.[16]

A few months went by. Her company had begun to make arrangements for her to work part-time. But one Sunday, as Angela was sitting in the church that her family attended sporadically, the strangest impression came upon her. She was to call the church and offer to work part-time. The idea completely blindsided her.

Never had any thought like this ever entered her mind. *After all*, she tried to reason, *what in the world would a church want with a marketing manager from a chemical company?* Despite the seeming lunacy of it, the impression of the idea in her head was so strong, the experience so unusual, and the idea so foreign to her that Angela reasoned this idea couldn't possibly be of her own making. Maybe it was from the Lord. Still, it took her three months to actually get around to contacting the church.

She sent an email to the church, admitting possible lunacy but wondering if there was a part-time opening for a person with her skills. Unbeknownst to her, the church leadership had just concluded that they needed someone to come help the church with marketing and communications, but were ready to dismiss the idea because it seemed too difficult to find someone competent enough in these areas who would be willing to work only part-time. And then Angela's résumé arrived.

When we hear a voice tell us to do something that we have never considered, or answer a question in a way that we could never have answered on our own, there is a strong possibility the Lord is speaking to us. Isaiah 55:8–9 reminds us that God's ways and thoughts are far beyond our ways and thoughts. Therefore, it makes sense that when God speaks to us, some of what he will say will never have even occurred to us before. God says as much in Isaiah 42:16, claiming, "I will lead the blind by ways they have not known; along unfamiliar paths I will guide them."

When God guided Samuel and Israel to look for Saul in the baggage, no one would have guessed that is where they would find the new king of Israel (see 1 Sam. 10:22). Likewise, when God answered Daniel's question concerning King Nebuchadnezzar's dream, Daniel realized that the answer must have come from God because the answer to the question could not have come from someone else (see Dan. 2).

When I was a senior in high school, most of my classmates at our public school were planning an all-night, post-prom party. I wanted to go more than anything in the world. Yet this was exactly the kind of thing my parents would never allow. Never.

My friends didn't even bother to egg me on. They knew getting permission was hopeless. Even my soft-hearted mother, who usually could be counted on to help me double-team my dad, refused to help on the grounds that it was pointless. But, hoping against hope, I pleaded with my dad. He gave me his usual answer: "I'll pray about it." Days went by. I had already resigned myself to hearing no, but the strangest thing happened. He said yes! I was incredulous. I didn't want to jeopardize my good fortune, but this was too amazing to let go. "What happened?" I blurted out.

"I was sure the answer was going to be no," my dad admitted, "but as I prayed about it, 'yes' kept coming to me. Over the past few days of prayer I have come to have a real peace about you going. God trusts you, and I can too." One of the ways my dad recognized God's voice was that it gave him an answer that was so unexpected. (Incidentally, this was the day I remember realizing that God must really speak to people, because there was no other reasonable explanation for this answer. It laid the foundation for much of what I later discovered about God's leading and guiding.)

Admittedly, this criterion for distinguishing God's voice is more prone to misunderstanding than the previous five. After all, I have lots of crazy ideas that pop into my head! Only sheer foolishness would attribute all of those to God simply on the basis that they are unexpected. However, one of the distinguishing characteristics of God's way of communicating is that he often says to us things that we have never thought of before or could not have come to on our own.

Conclusion

In C. S. Lewis's *Prince Caspian*, the four Pevensie children and Trumpkin the dwarf find themselves lost in Narnia on their way to find Prince Caspian. Aslan, the great lion, has not yet made an appearance in this book, though the children know him well from their previous adventure in Narnia. Standing beside a river, the group must choose to go upriver or down. Reasoning among themselves, they determine going downriver is the wisest choice. Just as they are about to leave, Lucy suddenly cries out,

"Look! Look! Look! . . . The Lion," said Lucy. "Aslan himself. Didn't you see?" . . . "Where, Lu?" asked Peter. "Right up there between those mountain ashes. No, this side of the gorge. And up, not down. Just the opposite of the way that you want us to go. And he wanted us to go up where he was—up there." "How do you know that was what he wanted?" asked Edmund. "He— I—I just know," said Lucy, "by his face."[17]

To say that God has a distinguishable and usually non-audible voice means that he has a way of communicating with us that becomes more and more recognizable the more we are acquainted with him. Some of the distinguishing features of his voice, as Lewis deftly illustrates, include the fact that he often speaks at unexpected times, saying unexpected things. He is usually telling us to trust him and to not follow what human wisdom tells us to do.

God has a distinguishable voice that he wants us to be able to recognize, something that becomes easier the more time we spend immersed in God's Word. No one chapter could identify all the distinguishing characteristics of God's voice, but we have at least seen six important ones. We are now ready to look at the process of how we go about listening for guidance from God.

Discussion Questions

1. When Jesus promises that his sheep will know his voice, what assurances does that provide you? How well would you characterize your current ability to recognize Jesus's patterns of communication?

2. Have you ever seen someone who thought God was telling them to do something, but it violated specific commands in the Bible? How did they handle the conflict between

what they thought God was saying and what the Bible actually said?

3. In this chapter we have seen different patterns describing how God communicates with us. What are other characteristics you have noticed about the way God speaks and acts?

the process
of listening

5

preparing to listen

If someone isn't ready to listen, *they won't hear what you are saying.*

Doctors know this. Salespeople understand this. Teachers get this. Parents resonate with this. Anyone who tries to communicate truth to another person should recognize the accuracy of this claim.

If a person visiting their doctor isn't ready to listen to the doctor's advice about their weight, they will not hear what the doctor is saying—no matter how loudly, forcefully, masterfully, convincingly, or often he or she says it.

Communication from God is similar. Of course, God can force someone to listen to him—but he usually doesn't. If we are going to hear from God, we must be prepared to listen to God.

The Key Text

James 1:5–7 says,

> If any of you lacks wisdom, you should ask God, who gives
> generously to all without finding fault, and it will be given to

you. But when you ask, *you must believe and not doubt*, because the one who doubts is like a wave of the sea, blown and tossed by the wind. That person should not expect to receive anything from the Lord. (emphasis mine)

The operative word here is *believe*. Without belief (or faith), no one's request for guidance from God will be answered. Practically speaking, this leads us to five questions each of us must honestly ask ourselves before we can expect to hear from the Lord.

Are You Pure in God's Eyes?

In the seventh year, in the fifth month on the tenth day, some of the elders of Israel came to inquire of the LORD, and they sat down in front of me. Then the word of the LORD came to me: "Son of man, speak to the elders of Israel and say to them, 'This is what the Sovereign LORD says: have you come to inquire of me? As surely as I live, I will not let you inquire of me,' declares the Sovereign LORD." (Ezek. 20:1–3)

Did you hear that? God categorically refused to provide guidance to Israel. He would not do it. He wouldn't even let them ask! Why not?

"When you offer your gifts—the sacrifice of your children in the fire—you continue to defile yourselves with all your idols to this day. Am I to let you inquire of me, you Israelites? As surely as I live," declares the Sovereign LORD, "I will not let you inquire of me." (v. 31)

Israel was enmeshed in wicked idolatry. What guidance they were seeking from God is unclear. What is crystal clear is God's adamant refusal to provide counsel. As with Israel, so with us. When James makes our hearing from the Lord dependent on our willingness to believe, he is not just saying we must believe God will respond. That is true, as we will see in just a minute, but there is much more to it than that. To believe God is to obey him, which is precisely James's point (see 2:14–26). And Paul's too, when he talks about the obedience that faith produces (see Rom. 1:5; 16:26). Lacking the faith to obey God, we stifle the Spirit's ability to communicate with us (see 1 Thess. 5:19). Wait a minute. We all sin, don't we? Of course. But there is a difference between irregular, discouraging slips into disobedience that are quickly repented of—even if they happen again—and blatant, unrepentant refusals to obey God. Sin always hinders our relationship with God, but those quickly repented of may only make God's voice more difficult to hear, while habitual, unconfessed, and rebellious sins can cause God to stop talking to us completely.

Let me illustrate. Suppose you wanted to sit down with the owner of the small company that you work for and get some career advice. Tuesday is your appointed meeting day. When Tuesday arrives, you are late. By an hour. For no good reason. The owner is agitated that he has been waiting for you, yet in general he considers you a wonderful employee. It is safe to say that before he would share his career advice with you, you should genuinely apologize for being late. Yet being late—as long as it comes with an apology—will not cause him to withhold his advice. If on the other hand you are not a good employee and have been recklessly embezzling money from the company—and the owner knows it—you should not expect him to share career advice with you. The only advice you should expect from him is, "Stop stealing money and make restitution!" So it is with God. If we are to receive guidance from God we must apologize for any disobedience currently in our lives, but habitual, unrepentant sin will render God silent except for one word: *repent.*

Now, I recognize that this can be tough to hear right out of the gate. Taken the wrong way, it can lead to a vicious cycle of soul-searching where we feel that we are never good enough to go to God. But that is not the point. God loves us and wants us to seek guidance from him. He does not expect perfection from us before he will speak. If you are right now cataloging any possible sins in your mind from years ago and disappointedly thinking that you're disqualified from asking for God's advice—stop. However, all of us should go through a process of honest soul-searching before God.

Frequently, I work through the material in this book with college students and young adults, who are often severely tempted with the sins of sexual immorality and pornography. I plead with them to consider the cost of engaging in these sins. Not only do such sins have a devastating effect on relationships both present and future, but they also greatly hinder our ability to receive counsel and guidance from God—a critical mistake at the worst possible time in life. Every choice that they make, whether regarding careers, education, spouses, singleness, or doing something radical for the Lord, will be cast into confusion because of the presence of these sins. Why would they—or why would we—want to so severely jeopardize their potential for a joyful, God-directed life? God is crystal clear in Ezekiel: he absolutely will not respond to those who are defiantly disobeying him.

The first step in preparing to listen to God is confessing and removing any areas of habitual, unconfessed sin.

Are You Willing to Do Whatever God Advises, No Matter What?

Randy and Lydia owned a 140-year-old jewelry store downtown. The store's location was rapidly beginning to hinder their ability to attract and retain customers. They felt faced with a choice: stay where the store had always been, or move to an available property outside the downtown area. Both choices carried risks and they desperately wanted God to help them with this decision. When they came to talk to me, one of the first questions I asked was, "Are you willing to do whatever God advises?" Thinking that meant "Are you willing to either stay downtown or move out to the suburbs?" they said, "Yes, of course." But that isn't what I meant. "What if God advises you to shut down the business, are you willing to do that?" Lydia, especially, was taken aback by this. That was not an option they had been considering. If you are going to ask God for counsel and advice, you have to be willing to do *whatever* he advises.

Remember, God is a better decision maker than we are. While all Christians will agree in principle with that point, whether we actually *believe* it in our heart of hearts makes all the difference in the world. If God is better at making decisions than we are, then when we seek guidance from God we will do so with the attitude of "not my will but yours be done." This is not a small point. Many people get tripped up here. Christians may hear about receiving guidance from God and think, *That's not a bad idea. I think I'll try it.* But they have already made up their minds as to what they want to do. In effect, they are simply asking God to ratify a decision, or choose between options they have preselected. God is not into rubber-stamping our already-made decisions. As Oswald Chambers said,

> We should get in the habit of continually seeking His counsel on everything, instead of making our own commonsense decisions and then asking Him to bless them. He cannot bless them; it is not in His realm to do so, and those decisions are severed from reality.[1]

To see the contrast between someone who has already decided what they want to have happen and someone who earnestly wants to hear from God, consider the story of Jehoshaphat and Ahab in 1 Kings 22. Jehoshaphat, the king of Judah, paid a visit to Ahab, the king of Israel. Ahab had made up his mind to attack Aram to try to retake Ramoth Gilead. Jehoshaphat was ready to agree, but said, "First seek the counsel of the LORD" (v. 5). I imagine that Ahab was annoyed by this request, but wanting to humor his ally he summoned four hundred prophets. When asked, all four hundred together told the king what he wanted to hear—he should attack Aram. But Jehoshaphat was suspicious because these prophets seemed to only say what the king wanted to hear.[2] So Jehoshaphat asked for a true prophet of the Lord. Ahab revealed that there was one, Micaiah, but—get this—"I hate him because he never prophesies anything good about me, but always bad" (v. 8). Jehoshaphat rebuked Ahab for his attitude, and Micaiah is summoned. At first Micaiah agreed with the assessment of the other prophets because he knew that this was what Ahab wanted to hear. Only when he was forced to swear to tell the truth did Micaiah actually reveal that Israel was going to get routed if they went into battle and Ahab would be killed. Rather than becoming afraid, Ahab turned to Jehoshaphat and snidely commented, "Didn't I tell you he never prophesies anything good about me, but only bad?" (v. 18).

Here are two contrasting perspectives. Ahab had already made up his mind. He wanted his decision to attack confirmed. Jehoshaphat, however, genuinely wanted to hear from the Lord. God's guidance and direction came only because of Jehoshaphat's attitude, and in spite of Ahab's. Unfortunately Jehoshaphat, blinded by Ahab, didn't recognize God's voice in the words of Micaiah. Tragically, he agreed to go off to war, where Israel and Judah suffered a massive defeat and Ahab died.

I have already mentioned that God arranged my marriage. Part of that process was a conscious decision to waive my right to choose my own spouse. I firmly believe that God gave me the freedom to marry whomever I chose, as long as she was a believer eligible for marriage. However, having no confidence in my ability to make a good decision on my own—after all, "a wife of noble character who can find?" (Prov. 31:10)—I turned to God and told him that I was waiving any right that I had to choose a spouse. If he wanted me to remain single, I would remain single. If he wanted me to wait ten years to get married, I would wait ten years. I resolved not to make any demands regarding appearance, background, interests, family, life goals, or anything else. Rather than taking the name of a particular girl to whom I might have been attracted to the Lord for his rubber stamp, I envisioned going to the Lord with a blank piece of paper and begging him in his grace, love, and infinite wisdom to write down the name of the person he was choosing. It was at that point I believe I was ready to hear directly from the Lord.

"Well," someone might reason, "perhaps we could seek God out and just see what he says. After all, if I don't like what he suggests I can simply not do it." This is not the right attitude, either. The nation of Israel tried this unsuccessfully in Jeremiah 42. They had already decided to flee from the Promised Land, but weren't sure where to go. So they came to Jeremiah and asked him to seek God's leading on what they should do. Jeremiah warned them: you cannot ask God's advice and then simply disregard it. Although they initially agreed to obey no matter what God told them, when Israel heard God tell them to stay in the land and not go to Egypt, they decided to do exactly the opposite of what God advised. Jeremiah tells them that they have made a fatal mistake by coming to ask and then not obeying. Better to not have asked at all than to ask for guidance and then disregard it.

God's advice is not subject to our approval. It is true that you and I can make decisions on our own without seeking advice and counsel from God. However, if God is going to provide guidance and advice, he expects it to be followed. For this reason, I believe, God usually shares his counsel only with those who have committed themselves to following it.

Randy and Lydia did hear from the Lord that they should move their store from its downtown location. For the past three years, they have followed God's leading even when it has been very difficult. Randy shared with me that the whole process has been about changing their orientation from "this is what I want" to "this is what God wants," a struggle that has challenged them to trust and rely upon God daily. Lydia commented that the process has involved coming to the end of herself. "Asking God what he wants is very humbling. You may hear things from God about yourself you don't like." Their business is being blessed as they continue to walk the path God has chosen, experiencing daily "manna" from heaven.

If you and I are going to hear from the Lord, we must reach the point of honestly committing ourselves to doing whatever the Lord guides us to do—no matter how seemingly crazy or painful, and no matter whether or not it was an option we were considering. As Lewis Sperry Chafer said, "His leading is only for those who are already committed to do as he may choose.

To such it may be said, 'God is able to speak loud enough to make a *willing* soul hear.' "[3]

Are You Willing to Abandon Plan B?

James says that the person who requests wisdom from God must believe and not doubt because the person who doubts is "double-minded" (see James 1:8). What does it mean to be double-minded? A double-minded person pursues two courses for guidance at the same time: God and something else. James is telling us we must not have a "plan B" in case God doesn't answer our prayers for guidance. For example, we might say to ourselves, *I am going to pray for two months and ask God to help me decide whether to enroll my children in Christian or public schools. If I don't hear anything from him then I am going to send my children to the Christian school like most of the other parents in my small group.* In this case, following the example of other parents in our small group is plan B in case God doesn't say anything. According to James, the existence of plan B in the back of our minds invalidates our request for guidance from God. Such a person should not think he or she will receive any wisdom from the Lord.

Legend has it that in 1519, Spanish conquistador Hernando Cortez landed in Mexico with more than five hundred soldiers and sailors in search of treasure. Looking to motivate his men to be fully committed to this one cause, he ordered them to burn their own ships, ensuring that there would be no going back. Such single-minded commitment to pursue one single course of action was an expression of great faith that their mission would be successful. When we determine to ask God for guidance, we must "burn the boats." There is no going back to our comfortable ways of deciding for ourselves. There must be no plan B.

Are You Willing to Wrestle with God and Wait for God?

Hebrews 11:6 explains another aspect of faith implicit in what James is saying: "Without faith it is impossible to please God, because anyone who comes to him must *believe* that he exists and *that he rewards those who earnestly seek him.*" This notion of earnestly seeking the Lord is reminiscent of Deuteronomy 4:29: "But if from there you seek the LORD your God, you will find him if you seek him with all your heart and with all your soul." Seeking the Lord does not mean casually mentioning to God once, in an offhanded way, that you wouldn't mind getting some advice. It means being wholeheartedly, energetically, and zealously devoted to wrestling with God, begging him for clear guidance.

The classic expression of such earnestness is Jacob wrestling with God, refusing to let go until God blessed him (see Gen. 32). This earnestness and diligence is to be a picture for us of wrestling with God in prayer—refusing to let go until God blesses us with his counsel and direction.

Jesus demonstrates this type of earnest devotion in seeking guidance from God in prayer. On the eve of his crucifixion, Jesus was in the Garden of Gethsemane. Pure hell waited for him the next day, and Jesus desperately wanted to know if there was any possible way he would not have to endure the cross. So great was his anguish that sweat fell from his face like drops of blood (see Luke 22:44). (It is interesting that Jesus casts out demons and heals disease without breaking a sweat. Yet when he prays to the Father for strength and guidance, it is the most vigorous, exhausting activity we see him doing!) This is real wrestling with the Father: begging and pleading for an answer. Such earnestness and diligence are signs of true faith in God, faith that God rewards with an answer—as he did for Jesus (see Heb. 5:7). Even though Jesus was told there was no other way, he still received an answer.

A good friend of mine was facing a monumental career decision that would impact not only him and his family, but thousands of other people. Two choices lay before him. Either would have been a good choice, humanly speaking, but my friend needed to hear from the Lord. So he took one lunch hour every week for a year to go to a chapel and pray for counsel from the Lord about his decision. That's earnestness and diligence.

Why does God allow the struggle for guidance to require such exhausting wrestling? One of the blessings of wrestling with God is that our desires, hopes, and dreams are forced into submission to God's plans and ideas. Great energy is necessary to bring our wills into line with God's, and that energy is supplied through wrestling with God. As a result we develop great community with God through this wrestling process.[4]

Diligently seeking the Lord not only means being willing to wrestle with God in prayer, but also—ironically—being willing to wait for God. Psalm 27 ties these themes together. David, longing for guidance because of those who are trying to harm him, says, "My heart says of you 'Seek his face!' Your face, LORD, I will seek. . . . Teach me your way, LORD; lead me in a straight path because of my oppressors. . . . Wait for the LORD; be strong and take heart and wait for the LORD" (vv. 8, 11, 14). While David waits he seeks; while he seeks he waits.

Waiting for the Lord is different than passing the time until God says something. There are active listening strategies—things we can do to put ourselves in a position to hear from God. Sometimes God provides counsel and guidance with relatively little effort on our part. Often, however, it requires blood, sweat, tears, and much time. Before you commit yourself to receiving guidance from God, you must ask yourself, *Am I willing to actively wait for God to respond and to work diligently to listen? Am I willing to give God the time to communicate his response according to his timing?*

If we are unwilling to put in that sort of earnest and diligent effort when required, we cannot expect to hear from God.

Do You Believe God Is a Good Communicator?

Hebrews 11:6 says that without faith it is impossible to please God, for we must *believe* both *that he exists* and that he rewards those who diligently seek him. Hebrews is not talking about accepting intellectual apologetic arguments about God's existence. It means believing God exists as he truly is. We are required to believe not in the notion of God, but in God himself—not the God we have conjured up in our minds, but the God who actually *is*.

John Stott reminds us that one of the principal aspects of God is that he loves to communicate: "The chief reason why people do not know God is not because he hides from them, but because they hide from him. People who are eager to share their thoughts with others we describe as 'communicative.' May we not accurately apply the same adjective to God?"[5]

God is eager to share his thoughts with us. Most Christians can affirm this. But what about the follow-up question: Is God a *good* communicator? In other words, will the reward for diligently seeking God be well-communicated guidance, or some mysterious, enigmatic, unintelligible sign?

When I was younger, I used to think of God's communication style as being like that of a wizard from a cartoon I used to watch. The wizard was supposed to be the guide for six young adults who had been transported into this magical realm. Yet he never seemed to be around when the kids needed him. He would appear randomly, speak in cryptic, mysterious riddles, and disappear right as the kids began to ask questions that might illuminate what he was saying. In the end, the kids were left to figure it out on their own, only to have their wizard guide appear at the end to confirm what they had already concluded.

Others might resonate with how the German playwright Goethe described God as a communicator:

> Indeed, the power which is eternal moves us imperceptibly, one way or another, in the direction of what is beneficial to us, of counsel, of decision, of completion, and, as if borne along, we reach our goal.[6]

In this scene from Goethe's *The Natural Daughter*, Eugenie comes to a monk, seeking guidance from God through him. According to Goethe's monk, God gets an "A" for guiding and directing, but an "F" for communicating, since his guidance is imperceptible!

While the answer to the question "Is God a good communicator?" has to be yes—after all, he's God, and being best at everything is part of the job description—if we are being honest, most of us don't truly believe God is a very good communicator. If you are like me, you tend to value clear, concise, and comprehensive communication. After all, when we go to our financial advisor for advice, we expect her to tell us something like, "step 1, you need to have an emergency fund covering six months' worth of expenses; step 2, you should contribute the maximum matched amount to your company's retirement plan; step 3, you should consider adjusting the ratio of stocks and fixed assets to bring it more in line with these recommended percentages. If I were you, I would buy these stocks and I would consider selling these assets." Then we expect her to take our questions, explain anything we didn't understand in simpler language, and invite us to contact her with any further questions we think of after we leave. That's good communication!

If God is such a great communicator, why doesn't he communicate like this? That's a complex question and it requires a complex answer. First, sometimes he does communicate this way. Chad and Paula are the proud parents of wonderful twin girls. As the girls were reaching school age, Chad and Paula began looking for a new house. The family earnestly prayed together that God would show them the right house to buy. One day Kennedy, one of the twins, announced that God had shown her that they were to buy the house with the purple door. Now purple was Kennedy's favorite color, so they mostly dismissed this as childish musings. Still, they had been praying, and Kennedy had never said anything like that before, so the purple door was not easily brushed aside. Within a few weeks of Kennedy's comment, Chad and Paula's realtor called them with a house she thought would be perfect. On paper everything looked great. With eager anticipation they prayed for guidance from God, got into the car, and drove to see the house. They walked up the path to the front door—a blatantly, unforgettably, unmistakably purple door! Today, hanging in the house—which they purchased—is a picture of that front door with this Bible verse: "This is what the LORD says—your Redeemer, the Holy One of Israel: 'I am the LORD your God, who teaches you what is best for you, who directs you in the way you should go'" (Isa. 48:17). I don't know how God could have been more clear, concise, and comprehensive than to say, "Buy the house with the purple door."

Sometimes, though, clear, concise, and comprehensive is not the best communication strategy. Take for example God's dealings with the Israelites and the land he promised them. He was as clear as he could possibly be, guiding them with a cloud by day and a pillar of fire at night, and leading them to the exact land he wanted to give them. He then instructed that they send spies into the land. When the spies returned and Israel was afraid, God reminded them through Joshua and Caleb that he was with them, guaranteeing their success.[7] But they would not listen. So God used a less direct communication strategy. For the next forty years God led them around the wilderness, feeding them daily with manna, keeping their shoes and clothes from wearing out, and protecting them from enemies—all for the purpose of communicating to them one message: that he is the Lord and he can be trusted (see Deut. 29:5–6). This turned out to be a much more effective communication strategy, albeit one that required a lot of patience. God often chooses this more silent method of communicating to us through deeds and circumstances so that we understand not only what we are supposed to do, but also that we have the faith to know God will enable us to do it.

If God's communication always came in accordance with our expectations, it would not require faith. But listening to God does require faith—faith that God is the best communicator—even when we might think at the moment the evidence proves otherwise. Without such faith, it is impossible to hear from God.

I Wish I Had Followed My Own Advice

This advice is easier said than done. For much of my adult life, I always wanted to write a book (be careful what you wish for!).

At the end of my schooling, an opportunity presented itself to publish my dissertation. When this happened, I noticed a spark of selfish ambition welling up within me, but I buried this deep in my heart. I knew I should seek guidance from the Lord, so I began to pray, but I was afraid that this spark of selfish ambition would cause God to tell me no. So I prayed halfheartedly, wanting God to rubber-stamp what I had already decided to do. Not surprisingly, I heard nothing from God. Undeterred, I decided to seek advice from others whom I thought could help make my desires a reality. I talked to my supervisor, contacted people in the academic publishing industry, and talked to other students who had published their work. Rationalizing that I was simply listening for God in their advice, I put my trust in them and followed what they told me to do. Through my assertiveness, I helped create an opportunity to publish the work with a reputable academic publisher. This was great—I was fulfilling a longtime dream.

However, looking back I can see the mercy and grace of God as he tried to encourage me down a different path with a different publisher. But the path he seemed to be suggesting required more patience, faith, and hard work. I would have to do a lot more revising, and even then it might not be accepted. Growing impatient, I told God that unless I heard otherwise I would assume I should seize the opportunity I had come up with. Convincing myself I had God's approval—why else would it be working out?—I barreled ahead. But God was not guiding the process. Looking back, I can see that now. While the book was published, the whole process felt very much like something I had facilitated, rather than being from the Lord. In hindsight, I wish I had followed the advice I have given you here. I regret not dealing with the sin of selfish ambition. I regret forgetting to embrace the not-my-will-but-yours attitude. I regret not waiting and wrestling with God. I regret having a plan B that allowed me to get what I wanted, even when I hadn't heard from God.

God speaks best when we have prepared ourselves to listen. If we make every effort to purify our lives of habitual sins, approach God with the right attitude, abandon any alternate courses of action, steel ourselves to earnestly wrestle with him in prayer, and believe that he can and will communicate with us, then we are ready to hear from him.

Discussion Questions

1. Can you think of an example when someone was not ready to listen to your advice? How did you help prepare them to listen to what you had to say? Has God ever done anything to get your attention and prepare you to listen to him?

2. To listen to God we must embrace purity, do whatever God advises, abandon "plan B," wrestle and wait for God, and believe he is a good communicator. Which of these five preparatory steps do you find easiest, and which is the hardest?

3. In this chapter, I gave an example of a time when I had not truly prepared myself to listen for God—instead it was my own voice I was hearing in my head. Has that ever happened to you? What were the circumstances in which that happened?

6

actively listening

*M*ondegreens. **Who knew** they had a name? Everyone has fallen victim to mondegreens—misunderstood song lyrics—at one time or another, whether singing in church or in the shower. My favorites include, "Excuse me while I kiss this guy" (should be "kiss the sky"); "there's a bathroom on the right" ("there's a bad moon on the rise"); and "fear the Lord and shove evil" ("fear the Lord and shun evil"—this one is courtesy of my youngest daughter!). This universal phenomenon highlights the difference between hearing and listening. *Hearing* is simply processing audible clues. *Listening* is an active process that seeks to assimilate communication. Hearing can happen by accident, as when we overhear a conversation on the subway or in the store. Listening never happens by accident. It is a conscious choice to engage in the process of receiving communication.

We cannot force God to speak his guidance to us. There is no formula to make it happen. But there are steps we can take to actively pursue listening to God for guidance.

Carve Out Time

Numerous scientific studies confirm what most of us know by sense: background noise from TV and music disrupt our brain's ability to focus.[1] Even more disturbing is a Stanford study showing that those who are constantly exposed to multiple media sources simultaneously damage their abilities to focus even when the distractions are not there![2] What all this means is that if we are going to hear from God, we need to carve out some time away from the ever-increasing noise of this world, whether texts, emails, talk radio, TV, blogs, smart phones, novels, friends, coffee-shop conversations, family, seminars, or whatever. Our ability to focus on listening to God is proportional to the amount of undivided attention we give him.

Jesus showed us this by example. His custom was to spend time alone with the Father in prayer (see Mark 1:35). He needed time away from the crowds to be alone with God (see Matt. 14:23). This is why Christians have emphasized the need for silence and solitude, especially when seeking guidance from God.

Start Reading

A primary way that God speaks is through his Word. But we cannot predict which passages he will speak to us through, or when it will happen. When we are looking for an answer to a question or seeking guidance, it is useful to set aside time to read through large portions of Scripture. If you are facing a difficult decision about whether to accept a job transfer that has been offered to you, sit down at the beginning of Mark's Gospel, for example, and begin reading. God may use a story from Scripture to speak to you in a new and fresh way. Try using different translations. A familiar passage your mind may subconsciously skip over can strike you in a new way in an unfamiliar translation. When I am seeking direction from the Lord, I block out time and try to read large sections of Scripture to see what the Lord causes to jump out at me. There have even been times when, over the course of a few weeks, I have sat down and systematically read the whole New Testament with a specific question in mind, trying to hear the voice of the Lord.

Cindy, who works for a local housing authority, described to me an experience of actively listening to God through Scripture. She writes:

> After interviewing applicants for the position of resident assistant/housemother, I was struggling to decide who would fit best. The last resident assistant hadn't worked out so well and I just knew I wanted God's wisdom. It truly was one of the first times I went to God through His Word, expecting specific direction.
>
> I didn't really have a clue what I was doing. It was before the days of my electronic Bible with its search function. Instead I took my study Bible and a concordance to the dining room table. My thinking was that as the Holy Spirit brought words and thoughts to my mind, I could look up specific passages and hear from the Lord. I remember sitting down at the dining room table and telling the Lord I didn't know what I was doing. I asked that He honor my attempts to seek His will. I felt a little bit bold (and odd) with my expectant attitude and faith that He wanted to answer me.
>
> Then I went to the concordance and looked up words that might be connected with the issue. I read passages and would think, "I like that, but I don't see the relevance." But a different word would pop up and seem relevant. So back to the concordance and more passages. I probably spent 2–3 hours at it. Some passages would seem connected, and I wondered what I was supposed to be "hearing" from those. But I didn't have any peace yet about the decision. Eventually I came to one that I didn't have to pat and shape into the answer I was seeking. The Holy Spirit just reverberated. It was a mental knowing, a spiritual peace and a physical resonating.[3]

Another strategy that many have found useful is to have a daily reading schedule of Scripture. It is uncanny how often God will speak through daily readings to answer a specific question that arises that particular day. In just the past six months, God has used my daily reading of Scripture to answer very specific questions and concerns I had about how I should respond to stressful situations and what the future held (specifically Psalms 27 and 91).

God will speak through his Scriptures if we give him the opportunity.

Fast and Pray

Ever wonder how biblical authors decided to write their books? The traditional story of how the apostle John decided to write the Gospel of John is a fascinating testament to the role of fasting and prayer in listening to God.

> When John's fellow disciples and bishops urged him to write, he said, "Fast with me from today for three days, and let us tell one another whatever will be revealed to us." In the same night it was revealed to Andrew, one of his apostles, that John should write down everything in his own name, while all of them should review it.[4]

Fasting is central to many passages of Scripture in which people are seeking advice from the Lord or preparing to hear from the Lord (see Neh. 1; 2 Chron. 20:3–4; Dan. 9; Acts 13:1–3). The Bible usually refers to fasting from food, but Jesus fasted from sleep when seeking the Father's guidance before choosing his twelve apostles (see Luke 6:12–16), and Paul mentions husbands and wives fasting from sex for the purpose of praying (see 1 Cor. 7:5).

If you have never fasted before there are several helpful books on the topic, such as *Celebration of Discipline* by Richard Foster. An easy way to begin fasting is to select a day. On the night before, refrain from eating anything after dinner. When you wake the next morning, don't eat any food until dinnertime. Take the time you normally would have spent eating, such as your lunch break, and spend that time praying and reading Scripture instead. During your time of prayer, focus specifically on the area in which you need guidance. When you pray, tell God how much you long to hear his counsel. Commit yourself to following his guidance, no matter what it might be. Repent of any sinful actions and attitudes. Ask him to purify your motives and enable you to submit to his leading. Promise to give him the glory when he does lead and guide. Admit your confusion. Be honest if you are getting frustrated. Take time to listen to what he might be saying. Write down any promptings you feel.

You can never pray too much or too urgently for counsel from God.

Listen to Those Who Listen

Some Christians excel at listening to God, whether because of their position, their giftedness, or their experience in recognizing God's voice.

Because of their positions, pastors and parents, for example, are often given guidance from the Lord to share with the people in their congregations or with their children. Remember, God supports the social structures of church and family he has ordained. God, who communicates through love, also speaks through pastors and parents because these people should love and care for us most deeply, under normal circumstances.

There are also other people who seem to always be in tune with what God is saying. It might be because they have a spiritual gift of wisdom, faith, or discernment, or perhaps because they are further along in the process of learning to recognize God's voice. Whatever the reason, I do know that certain people seem to hear from God more than others. In my life, one of these people is a godly, older man in our church. I usually seek his advice when I am trying to hear from God. Anytime he comes to me with something to share, I drop whatever I am doing so that I can pay close attention.

Are there people like this in your life? Sit down with them and talk through your situation. Be honest about your struggles and confusion. Listen carefully to what they say, for in their voice you might hear a word from the Lord.

Identify the "Fingerprints of God"

Many times when we are looking for God's guidance, we are like detectives looking for clues. God is always at work in our lives, and we can look for evidences of his handiwork.

Tyler had just completed his freshman season as the backup quarterback at an NCAA Division I school. Frustrated with his lack of playing time and the possibility of sitting on the bench for another two years, Tyler began to wonder if God might be leading him to transfer to another school. As he and I talked through the process, I asked him to describe for me what was happening in his life as he considered this decision. He shared with me that one of his roommates had just decided to transfer to the same school Tyler was considering. That "coincidence" seemed mildly noteworthy. Tyler also told me that he had contacted a Division II school about their potential interest in adding him to their roster and they seemed very eager. I told him not to put too much weight on that, since it seemed natural rather than supernatural that a lower division school would be interested in Tyler coming to play for their team. Tyler also told me that two weeks prior to our conversation, he had a vivid dream in which his recently deceased grandmother, who had played a big role in his spiritual development, was urging him to transfer. To me that was quite noteworthy. One big mark against transferring was that his parents, although supportive of his decision, were not for it. We went through other remembrances, trying to identify God's fingerprints. At the end of our conversation, we had identified a number of clues as to God's leading. Almost all of them—except, significantly, his parents' opinion—pointed toward Tyler transferring schools. Soon after, Tyler called the coach to ask for his transfer papers.

As you look for the fingerprints of God, talk through your findings with another Christian. Sometimes we overlook significant clues. The converse is true as well. Others may have information or a perspective that changes our perspective on whether or not an event bears God's fingerprints. Consider the fictitious illustration of Bob, a marketing specialist at a large company. Suppose Bob wanted to be assigned to a new product development project at his company. When Bob's boss offered it to him unsolicited, Bob took this as a clue that this might be from God, since he did not campaign for or request the assignment. However, when Bob excitedly tells his co-worker Jack the news, Jack reveals that everyone knew Bob wanted that assignment. He had been dropping subtle clues for months. The boss gave Bob the assignment because he knew that would make Bob happy. This additional information that Jack provides should temper how strongly Bob considers his boss's offer as a fingerprint of God.

Another hint when trying to discover the fingerprints of God is to look for some connection to things you are sure God was involved in before. For example, if you came to faith ten years ago during college and now your pastor asks if you would be willing to volunteer with the college ministry, that may very well be from the Lord. Or if God called you to work at a non-profit to help them implement a new software system and three years later, just as the project is winding down, another opportunity presents itself, that may well be a fingerprint of God's leading encouraging you to pursue that other opportunity.

Conversely, if during a time of fasting and prayer God spoke to you, telling you to join a medical practice and confirming it through pretty amazing circumstances, I wouldn't leave years later simply if another practice came along and offered more money. I would expect that if God was leading, he would do something as compelling to move you out of your practice as he did to get you in.

Or perhaps you've been struggling with your relationship with God and you wake up one morning feeling compelled to visit a new church. During that service you feel as if the sermon was written specifically for you. Brimming with questions, you go down front to speak to the pastor. While you are talking with him, a random person happens to be walking by, and the pastor grabs him and says, "I want you to meet Jacob. He is going through exactly what you are. You two should get together for lunch." Jacob takes your number and actually calls to set something up. At lunch you really hit it off. Jacob invites you to join his small group Bible study. At that point, given that God seemed to compel you to go to church that morning, spoke to you through the sermon, and arranged a "chance" meeting with Jacob—all fingerprints of God—I would strongly consider that God is telling you to join the small group.

To help with this detective work, some people find it useful to keep a journal when they are looking for guidance from God.

Take Note of Ideas

Ben Johnson wisely advises:

> When even casual ideas come to your consciousness, pause and wonder where they came from. And notice especially those ideas that come unexpectedly and with great clarity. If they persist, give them extra attention.[5]

A friend felt led by God to give a considerable sum of money to a specific overseas mission work. Doing all the due diligence one could reasonably expect, he gave the money. Within ninety days it was all gone, having been stolen by some wolves in sheep's clothing. As soon as he heard the deeply distressing news, the ridiculous idea popped into his mind to replace the money. Really? Could this possibly be from God? He tried to brush the idea aside, but it persisted day and night until he wrote the ministry another check for the same amount.

Of course, we all have ideas that stick around in our brains that are not from the Lord. But one of the ways we actively listen for God's voice is to take the time to think through those ideas that have come into our minds. Ask yourself the question, *Where would such an idea come from?* In the case of my friend who gave the money—twice—was it possible that this was his own idea? Was Satan (or spiritual forces of darkness) behind this idea? Or might it actually be from God? To my friend, this seemed like just the kind of crazy thing God would tell him to do. So he wrote a second check for the exact same amount. Later he found out that the people in the mission had been praying day and night for him to do so.

Go to Church

Kevin was kneeling in the front of church during a time of sermon reflection and prayer. He was sobbing. He had just come from the hospital, where his pregnant wife had been admitted because of preterm labor. Kevin and his wife had experienced struggles with pregnancy and newborns twice before. Their first child had miraculously lived; the second baby had tragically died. This time Kevin was kneeling and praying, asking God for mercy, guidance, and help. Kevin recalls that exact moment, describing it this way: "I began to panic as the first song ended. The song 'In Christ Alone' would be too perfect a match to the sermon. I was sure the song would play and was wondering what God was trying to tell me if it did." Kevin was panicked because "In Christ Alone" had been his and his wife's song of comfort when their second child died. He continued, "But that song never played. God had something different to tell me." The song that the congregation began to sing was "Great Is Thy Faithfulness." Kevin's grandparents were missionaries for fifty years and this song was their favorite hymn. Kevin used the song when sharing his testimony. Even more significantly, Kevin and his wife played that hymn at the dedication of their first child, the one God had miraculously protected. "God sung me, 'Great Is thy Faithfulness' as I kneeled. He chose to take me back not to my son's recent death, as I feared he would do, but rather to my first son's life and miraculous health." Kevin then added, "I found out when I got home that my wife was coming home, and the baby was just fine!"

If we want to hear God's voice, we should go where he is speaking. And God speaks in church. When God's people gather together as the church community in a worshiping assembly,

God is uniquely present and his voice is heard.[6] When you are seeking guidance from God, engage in corporate worship and see what happens. I don't mean sit in the back of the church and halfheartedly try to stay awake. I mean go down front, away from distractions, and fully engage. Listen. Take notes. Examine the words of the songs. Pay close attention during testimony time. One of the great things about a worship service is that we are not in control. We usually did not pick the songs, the sermon, or the Scripture readings—meaning worship services are safe from our inner voice sabotaging the process. After all, if the Scripture reading at church this week is about paying fair wages and you are wrestling with whether to give pay increases to your employees, that is probably God answering your question.

In addition to participating in worship services, actively engaging in the life of the church can also be a means God uses to speak to us. Stanley Hauerwas, a prominent American theologian, tells the story of needing guidance from God as to whether to move from Notre Dame to Duke University. He says,

> I had been given one week to come to a final decision. I think I was finally able to accept the position because of the church. After I had come back from the interview at Duke, I told the folks at Broadway [his church] about my situation at Notre Dame and that I might receive an offer from Duke. I asked them to pray for us. I told them that I would do what they told me to do. God knows whether I was serious or not. After I received the call and letter officially offering me the position, I told the church that I now had to make up my mind and my mind was in their hands. We prayed for guidance. They told me after much discussion that they thought it a good thing for me to go to Duke.[7]

So he went.

If You Had to Guess . . .

Sometimes it is not until we are forced to articulate what God seems to be doing that his guidance becomes clear to us. I find it useful to ask myself and others the question: "If at this moment you had to say which way God was moving, what would you say right now and why?" Sometimes this question is asked too early in the process. God may not have said anything yet. Other times this is a useful question because God gives us a subjective sense of which way he is guiding and directing us. When a question like this forces the issue, these subjective feelings can come to the surface.

All of the Above

So which of these avenues for listening to God should you pursue? If it is possible to draw a positive point from a negative example, consider Saul in 1 Samuel 28. He was desperate to hear from the Lord regarding the invasion of the Philistines. Verse 6 says Saul "inquired of the LORD, but the LORD did not answer him by dreams or Urim or prophets."

God refused to answer Saul, but the positive point is that Saul pursued multiple ways of hearing from the Lord. Three are listed: dreams, prophets, and something known as the Urim. Likewise, in Acts 15 the leaders of the Jerusalem church both tried to identify the fingerprints of God and searched the Scriptures to hear God's voice. In both cases multiple approaches were taken to hear from the Lord.

So which of these strategies should you pursue for listening to God? As many as necessary.

A Great Example

It is fitting to close this chapter with a story from the pages of George Müller's diary. Müller, a nineteenth-century Christian evangelist and pastor who ran children's orphanages in England, was seeking God's guidance (he often calls it "God's will") as to whether to open another orphanage. In this story, the process of actively listening for God is well illustrated.

145

The process began when Müller acknowledged he wanted God's counsel and not his own thoughts.

> By the grace of God my heart says: Lord, if I could be sure that it is Thy will that I should go forward in this matter, I would do so cheerfully; and, on the other hand, if I could be sure that these are vain, foolish, proud thoughts, that they are not from Thee, I would, by Thy grace, hate them and entirely put them aside.

He pointed out that he has not come to consider building another orphanage because there has been an excess of money, indeed at that point the work was going through some very lean weeks where little money was coming in.

Six days later, Müller wrote,

> During the last six days, since writing the above, I have been, day after day, waiting upon God concerning this matter. It has generally been more or less all the day on my heart. When I have been awake at night, it has not been far from my thoughts.

He also decided not to tell anyone about this idea, even his wife:

> Moreover, hitherto I have not spoken about this thing even to my beloved wife, the sharer of my joys, sorrows, and labours for more than twenty years; nor is it likely that I should do so for some time to come: for I prefer quietly to wait on the Lord, without conversing on this subject, in order that thus I may be kept the more easily, by His blessing, from being influenced by things from without.

Fifteen days later Müller was beginning to get a sense from God that he should go forward with this project, but listen to how he described getting there:

> Every day since [the last entry] I have continued to pray about this matter, and that with a goodly measure of earnestness by the help of God. There has passed scarcely an hour during these

days, in which, whilst awake this matter has not been more or less before me. . . . This evening I have had again an especial solemn season for prayer, to seek to know the will of God. But whilst I continue to entreat and beseech the Lord, that He would not allow me to be deluded in this business, I may say I have scarcely any doubt remaining on my mind to what will be the issue, even that I should go forward in this matter.

Müller declared he was willing to wait for as long as it took to hear clearly from the Lord. He then commented honestly about his motives:

This calmness of mind, this having no will of my own in the matter, this only wishing to please my Heavenly Father in it, this only seeking His and not my honour in it; this state of heart, I say, is the fullest assurance to me that my heart is not under a fleshly excitement, and that, if I am helped thus to go on, I shall know the will of God to the full. But, while I write this, I cannot but add at the same time, that I do crave the honour and the glorious privilege to be more and more used by the Lord.

Another week passed, during which Müller heard God speaking to him through his reading of Proverbs, in particular 3:5–6; 11:3; and 16:3. Finally he concluded he had received guidance from the Lord:

My heart is more and more coming to a calm, quiet settled assurance, that the Lord will condescend to use me still further in the orphan work. Here Lord is Thy servant.[8]

Discussion Questions

1. What strategies or techniques make someone good at listening? How might these strategies or techniques make us better at listening to God?

2. When I share tips for seeking God's guidance, one of the most helpful images I have found is the idea of looking

for the fingerprints of God. What do you think of this idea? What does this image evoke in your mind about discovering God's guidance?

3. Have you ever pursued any of these strategies for actively listening for God? What was the result?

7

lessons learned

Learning to listen to God is a journey. As with any journey, there are lessons to learn along the way. Some I have learned from my own experience, and others I have picked up from those on the journey with me.

All at Once

Single! Jesus, Paul, and me. That was my plan. At some point during my undergraduate years, I made a decision that I would not seek marriage unless God specifically guided me in that direction. A few years passed, and I found myself in graduate school. Still adhering to my "single-first" philosophy, I suddenly noticed that I was being bombarded on all sides with the idea of marriage. God was speaking to one of my best friends, Aaron, regarding his future wife, and Aaron talked constantly to me every evening about what God was telling him. My pastor began a sermon series on the family and was focusing on singlehood and marriage. To top it off, I was given an assignment in one of my classes to study Ephesians 5:22–33 and write a twenty-page paper on God's view of marriage. For a few weeks, all day, all evening, and every weekend, all I ever heard about was marriage! Through my friend, my pastor, and my study of God's Word, I began to sense God was guiding me toward marriage. God was using each of these concurrent events—especially my study of Ephesians 5—to transform my view of marriage and incline my heart to desire to be married.

In this I learned a lesson that many other Christians have also learned: God often says the same thing through many different means at the same time.

Priscilla Shirer, who happens to be a friend from those graduate school days and the daughter of the pastor whose sermons were shaping my thoughts about marriage, recently wrote a book entitled *Discerning the Voice of God*. Priscilla shares quotes from Ben Carson and Steve Farrar that make the same point: "I know the Lord is speaking to me when He repeats the same message through many different venues in a short period of time," and "When I hear the same thing from two or three different people in a very short period of time, I know the Lord is speaking to me."[1]

An Intermediate Step

Tyler, the young football player I mentioned in the previous chapter, did not end up transferring schools. Having evaluated all the evidence and seen that it pointed to transferring, Tyler made an appointment to share the news with his soon-to-be former head coach, who then tried to convince Tyler to stay. Emboldened by his decision to transfer, Tyler began to respectfully share things with the head coach that he probably would not have told him otherwise. The coach, glad for his honesty, handed him the transfer papers to sign. Suddenly, Tyler reports, there was an overwhelming, inexplicable sense from God that he was not to transfer. "I knew beyond a shadow of a doubt at that moment that I was to remain at that school."

Had Tyler misinterpreted the fingerprints of God in thinking he was supposed to transfer? Possibly. Perhaps God used those fingerprints to see if Tyler would be obedient, but at the last minute stopped him from actually carrying through with it, much like Abraham not sacrificing his son Isaac. Or perhaps God used Tyler's decision to transfer as a way of getting him to engage with his coach at a different level so that they could have a more frank conversation. We are still waiting to see what God is doing in Tyler's life, but it seems that in order to get Tyler to the point of certainty that he should not transfer, God had to use the intermediate step of guiding him toward transferring.

One day, I was sitting down to write a sermon. While praying and asking God for an illustration, a strong feeling popped into my head to use the story of an old friend of mine named Matt. Because I hadn't thought about this friend in a few years, and because it came during a time of prayer in response to a specific request for help, I took this as being from the Lord. As I tried to write out my friend's story, there were some details that I couldn't quite remember. Contacting Matt, I told him what I was doing and asked if we could chat. Confident that I had heard from the Lord, I began to try to guide Matt into framing his story in such a way that it would be perfect for the sermon. However, the more I talked to him the less the story actually seemed to fit. Sensing my confusion, Matt asked me about my sermon. He listened for a few minutes, and then said, "Why don't you use the movie *Les Miserables* as your illustration? It's perfect for what you are trying to say."

I politely thanked him, hung up the phone, and silently dismissed his suggestion as unworkable. But his suggestion kept popping into my mind until finally I gave in and tried to use it. I ended up rewriting the whole sermon around the illustration. It was perfect.

Why didn't God just tell me to use *Les Miserables* while I was praying? The musical is one of my favorites, and I am always recommending the movie version to others. Did God want me to contact Matt for some reason in order to hear it from him? Was there something God wanted to communicate to Matt? I am not sure, but it seemed to me that God guiding me to Matt was somehow a necessary intermediate step on the way to the final destination.

This is why the process of talking through what we think we have heard from God with others is so important. It is possible that God prompts you to consider sending your children to a different school in order to spur a discussion with your wife about how to better equip your children to succeed at the school they currently attend.

Does this make God deceitful? No. In the examples mentioned above, God had not definitely stated his guidance only to change course later. Instead he used thoughts and means to lead us toward his true guidance. How do we know when God is leading us toward an idea that is merely a means to an end instead of the end itself? This is God's responsibility to make clear to us, if we have honestly sought his guidance. Our responsibility is to remain open to the possibility that God may be working in this way in our lives.

Decisions Made in Faith

What about the times when God does not provide "writing on the wall," with no jaw-dropping circumstances, no overwhelming sense that we are to do one thing over another, or no clearly answered fleece? Many times in my life I have been nearly 100 percent sure that God had guided in one way or another. At other times there wasn't anything more than a subjective sense that something was from the Lord. Does that mean God has not spoken?

One reassuring principle can be drawn from the idea in Scripture that we walk by faith, not by sight. If you have searched out the Lord and listened for his guidance as best you can, choose the path you think he is leading you down—even though you do not have absolute certainty—and you will be making the decision *in faith*.

Listen to the way George Müller described it:

> The child who has again and again besought His Heavenly Father not to allow him to be deluded, nor even to make a mistake, is at peace, perfectly at peace concerning this decision; and has

thus the assurance that the decision come to, after much prayer during weeks and months, is the leading of the Holy Spirit; and therefore purposes to go forward, assuredly believing that he will not be confounded, for he trusts in God.[2]

Sometimes my confidence level that God is in something is just barely above 50 percent, but to go with what you think God is telling you to do is an act of faith, and God works through acts of faith. Of course, it is easy to cheat the system here—to skip praying, skip earnestly seeking God, skip everything else I have been talking about, and simply assume your first hunch of what to do is from God. That is not a decision made in faith.

Could My Wife Be Wrong?

My wife can be like Ahithophel. Remember him? Getting advice from him was like getting advice from God (see 2 Sam. 16:23). God has gifted my wife in amazing ways, especially with regard to critiquing sermons and messages. So good is her advice that early on I learned it was better to get it before I preached a sermon, rather than afterwards. She now reads through each sermon before I preach it, and makes suggestions. Almost universally, I heed her advice. Of the few times I have disregarded her advice, I regretted doing so. Except once.

Given the singular nature of this event, it is etched in my memory. The text of my sermon was 1 Corinthians 10:13. During a day of fasting and prayer for the service, I came upon the idea of closing the sermon with a skit to illustrate the main point of the sermon. When I shared this idea with my wife, she advised against it. When I was ready to discard the idea, God began to bombard me with evidence that I was to use this creative element. The more I prayed, the more confident I became that God was telling me to use it. I became confused. I began to plead with God for more clarity. During that time I began to sense that while God normally provided guidance through my wife, I was beginning to rely on her rather than on God speaking through her. For this reason, he pressed heavily upon me during prayer, through circumstances, and with affirmation from others that I was to use this element to end the sermon. With fear and trembling I went ahead and did what my wife advised me not to do. In the end, God used the sermon in great ways to communicate his truth to the congregation. The uniqueness of this event affirmed that my wife is a gift from God to guide me in these types of decisions, but ultimately it is God whom I must trust for wisdom and guidance.

If you have a person in your life whose advice to you is like hearing from God himself, I am confident that at some point God will guide you to do something contrary to what that trusted advisor tells you to do. This is because God wants our trust to be in him—and him alone.

What a Fool! What a Fox!

Does everyone think that your decision is good and wise? It is probably not from the Lord, then. What? Yes, I meant that. If everyone thinks a path you are headed down is good and wise, then it is probably not the Lord who is leading and guiding you. That's because the wisdom of God, which the Spirit provides, is foolishness to the world (see 1 Cor. 1–2). So if God is leading, someone is going to think the decision is foolish.

Surely this means just non-Christians, doesn't it? Unfortunately, Paul's purpose in 1 Corinthians 1–2 is to rebuke the Corinthian Christians for thinking like non-Christians despite the fact that they have the Spirit. We experience this today as well. When Christians who are thinking with the world's values and world's mind-set hear what God has advised us through the Spirit to do, they also will think it to be foolishness.

For example, a Christian small-business owner who had always run his business with the strictest of standards for his employees came across a situation where an employee had made a series of bad ethical decisions. In the past, the businessman would have fired her immediately. But just prior to him learning of the employee's bad decisions, God had miraculously opened up a business deal that allowed his company to avoid going bankrupt, and the businessman was being drawn closer and closer to God. Inexplicably, he began to feel that firing this employee was not what God was leading him to do. As he consulted with others, they told him he was a fool for keeping her. He himself felt as if this decision contradicted the received wisdom of his past experiences, but he decided not to fire her. Was this from the Lord? It seems to have been.

When we follow the Lord's guidance, someone—usually non-Christians or immature Christians—will think what we are doing is foolish.

Sometimes, however, the opposite will happen. Instead of thinking us foolish, some people will assume that we are crafty and manipulative. The reason for this is that when God is guiding, he causes things to work together in such a way that the only explanation for some people is that we have been working behind the scenes to manipulate the process. That's what happened to King David. God had been guiding David, telling him precisely where to go and what to do. As a result David escaped from Saul's clutches in pretty remarkable ways, and the only explanation for those who had not experienced God's guidance in this way was voiced by Saul when he said, "Find out where David usually goes and who has seen him there. They tell me he is very crafty" (1 Sam. 23:22). But David wasn't crafty. The text makes clear he had no idea what to do, but depended on God's guidance and direction. Still he was accused of being crafty.[3]

Just in Time

But I have to know what to do by February 19, and God hasn't said anything yet! Earlier I told the story of needing to hear from God about what to do when I graduated from the University of Michigan. One of the most valuable lessons I learned from that experience was that God knows how to take into consideration the deadlines we face for decisions we have to make.

In my case, I pursued various occupational and educational opportunities, thinking God would open one door and close all the others. However, by February 19, 1995, not only were all my doors still open, but the day of decision for more than one opportunity had arrived.

Why hadn't God spoken yet? Didn't he know that I had to know something by February 19? It was at this point I made the fateful decision I mentioned earlier: it was guidance from God, or nothing. If he hadn't spoken, then I couldn't answer. Sheepishly, I called the company representatives to tell them I didn't know if I could accept their job offer yet. (Indecision is hardly an endearing quality for corporations looking for strong leaders.) Surprisingly, they were understanding. Each asked for a final, firm deadline. I picked a date out of the air that seemed far away at the time, but not too far: March 16. They all agreed that this would be fine.

By March 12, I was worried again. Still nothing, even when I had given God another month! Yet, incredibly, on March 13 God started to speak. By March 15 God had made it crystal clear that I was to move to Texas and take a job with Texas Instruments.

And with that I learned a valuable lesson: God understands how deadlines work. February 19 was not a hard and fast deadline, though I didn't know it at the time. March 16 was firm, even though I had picked it randomly. God's guidance arrived just in time.

Sometimes we think of God relaxing on his throne in heaven, safely outside the burdens of time, blissfully unaware of the pressures and deadlines we are facing in our lives. Nothing could be further from the truth. In 2 Chronicles 20, God understands that Jehoshaphat needs an answer immediately because the enemy is bearing down on him. And he gives him an immediate answer. In Daniel 2 God knows Daniel needs an answer before the end of the night. And he gives an answer before the end of the night. But our sense of urgency and timing is not always accurate. Sometimes God asks us to wait when we are seeking guidance because he is doing other things in other people's lives that affect what he advises us to do. Sometimes it is for the purpose of growing our faith. No matter what the reason, I have learned that God answers our requests for guidance in his timing, not in ours, but he always takes into account the pressures and deadlines that we are facing.

The Major Dissuasion

"And now, compelled by the Spirit, I am going to Jerusalem." This was Paul's claim in Acts 20:22. Ah, it must be nice to have such certainty and clear direction. Unfortunately, this peace couldn't have lasted long. When Paul arrived at Tyre, the believers there urged Paul "through the Spirit" (see 21:4) *not* to go to Jerusalem. What? Wasn't the Spirit telling Paul to go to Jerusalem?

Worse yet, at their next stop in Caesarea, a prophet came down from Judea and prophesied: "The Holy Spirit says, 'In this way the Jews of Jerusalem will bind the owner of this belt and will hand him over to the Gentiles.'" When Luke and the rest of the Christians heard this, they pleaded with Paul not to go to Jerusalem (Acts 21:11–12).

How difficult and confusing this must have been for Paul! All the believers he came into contact with, including his traveling companions, were urging him not to go to Jerusalem. And they were doing so, "through the Spirit!" Now, I do not think that the Spirit is contradicting himself, but more likely is revealing to these other believers how much Paul was going to suffer in Jerusalem. Yet the fact that he was going to suffer didn't mean he shouldn't go or that it wasn't from the Spirit. But surely this had to be disconcerting for Paul to have everyone—including those who were themselves hearing from the Spirit—totally against what he thought the Spirit was telling him to do.

In my own experience, I have found that this is a typical pattern for those who are listening to God. After you have heard from God, something major will happen to dissuade you from obeying or thinking you have heard correctly.

My friend Vernon had just such a dissuasion occur to him. For a long time, Vernon's heart was restless at his current job. He was longing to spend his time serving God in full-time ministry. He sensed this was from the Lord and his wife readily confirmed this. She eagerly began to encourage Vernon to pursue going into ministry.

Emboldened by the knowledge that the Lord was leading, Vernon signed up for a night class at a local seminary. Expecting to love it, he was shocked at how much he hated it. He felt out of his league, was intimidated by the amount of reading, and was not as interested in the subject matter as he thought he would be. Where was the confirmation from the Lord regarding his leading? Had he misheard what God was saying? Shaken, Vernon began to believe that God was not calling him into ministry after all.

Months passed, and Vernon found himself sharing his story with a trusted friend. This lesson—that after God calls you there will be a major dissuasion—was shared with Vernon. At once, he began to realize that this was a typical pattern in hearing from God. Discerning what had happened in the seminary class, Vernon and his friend were able to talk through how God would not use fears of inadequacy to tell Vernon he had not heard his calling correctly. Instead, this was a last-ditch effort from the Enemy to dissuade Vernon from obeying the Lord's leading.

Knowing that a major obstacle is most likely coming is often helpful for people, but my experience is that people are usually still looking for something small, a little speed bump on the road. More likely, the event will have the feeling of being a dead end, a kick in the gut, or a "you had better sit down for this one."

A Problem-Free Life?

When God leads and guides, everything goes perfectly, right?

That was the expectation floating around the nation of Israel in Judges 20. One of the tribes of Israel, Benjamin, had committed a terrible crime. The other eleven tribes gathered together to mete out punishment. Knowing they needed God's guidance, they asked him who should attack Benjamin first. God responded, "Judah is to go first." So Judah promptly went out . . . and was totally routed! They lost! It wasn't even close. Twenty-two thousand Israelites died. If God was guiding, shouldn't they have won?

Dazed and confused, the Israelites wept before the Lord until evening. How could this have happened? Had they misunderstood God? Again they inquired of the Lord. This time instead of asking who should go first, they asked an even more basic question, "Should we go and fight the Benjamites?" God responded, "Yes. Go fight them." Here now, for a second time, was the clear leading of the Lord. Confident, the children of Israel went into battle . . . and lost again! This time it was eighteen thousand men who died. Didn't God tell them to go to battle? Weren't they trying to punish wickedness? If God was guiding them, how could they lose?

This was unprecedented. Israel was dumbfounded and flabbergasted. In despair, the whole nation gathered at Bethel. This time they fasted, prayed, wept, and offered all sorts of sacrifices. For the third time they inquired of the Lord, begging and pleading for direction. "Should we go up to battle against Benjamin, or not?" Their newly added "or not," was dripping with doubt. God replied, saying, "Go. For this time I will give them into your hands."

And Israel was then victorious.

Wow. Twice God clearly led them and the result was defeat. Nothing in the text of Judges 20 gives any indication that God was displeased with Israel; there is no indication that they asked him incorrectly or misunderstood what he was saying. Only in God's third response do we realize that, while he was leading them the first two times, he had not promised them immediate victory.

Lest we think this story in Judges an anomaly, remember that in the first instance God led Moses to confront Pharaoh, Israel ended up having to make bricks without straw and angrily disowned Moses. When God led Hosea to marry Gomer, he led him into a marriage with a highly dysfunctional wife who cheated on him repeatedly. God led Ezekiel to be a prophet and then took his wife, the delight of his eyes, from him as part of his role as prophet. When God led Paul to Jerusalem, imprisonment was waiting for him. When God led Jesus to the cross, he led him to the place of inexplicable torment.

Earlier I told of God giving me my PhD dissertation topic at the very end of an all-night prayer session. What I didn't tell you is that I couldn't wait to go and share this idea with my supervisor. If God gave it to me, then my supervisor was going to think it was brilliant. Maybe he would even think I was brilliant! He didn't. He hated the topic. He told me not to do it. But, he conceded, if this were something that I really wanted to do, he would allow it.

But this was not the end of the difficulty with this topic. At one point, sitting in my apartment, my supervisor told me that he disliked one chapter I had written so much that perhaps I should reconsider whether I was cut out for doctoral studies. This is not something you want to hear after you have sold all your possessions and moved your wife overseas to get your PhD.[4]

So, too, there have been couples led to adopt children through an open adoption, where years later the child went back to their biological parents. There have been people encouraged by God to move overseas to do missions work only to have their spouse victimized in that foreign country.

When we let God choose our cars, it doesn't mean they will always be of the highest quality and never break down. When God selects material for us to teach, it doesn't mean teaching that material will be easy. When God chooses our spouse, it doesn't mean we will have a conflict-free marriage. Seeking guidance from God does not mean our decisions will result in a problem-free life. But when we yield our desires to his, we end up with the best possible path because God is wiser than we can ever fathom, loves us more than we love ourselves, and is working all things together for the glory of his name.

Changing Circumstances

Sometimes the circumstances that God uses to communicate may not last. For example, I have shared details of the story of how God moved me to Texas to take a job with Texas Instruments (TI) and attend Dallas Seminary upon graduation from university. One of the means God used to confirm this direction was the discovery that one of my former roommates and close friends had just recently moved to Dallas. *What are the odds?* was the thought that ran through my head. As I feared moving to a new place where I didn't know anyone, the thought of my friend being there set my mind at ease. We made plans to live together. At the time, I listed this living situation as one of the major evidences that God was leading me in this direction. I accepted the job at TI and began to make plans to move to Dallas. My friend found a place where we could live on the campus of a local university, with some other guys who were students there.

My friend signed the lease and started living there. The plan was that I would be added to the lease nearer to my move-in date. In the meantime, however, the university changed their policy. Only one non-student was now allowed per campus apartment. Living there suddenly was no longer an option for me. Worse still, my friend had already signed his lease and couldn't get out of it.

Discouraged, I found myself on the phone with Dallas Seminary a week or so later, asking for advice about classes. The person I spoke with suggested that working full-time and attending class part-time would go much smoother if I lived in a seminary dorm. Was this possible? I had assumed that only full-time students could live in the dorm. But Lincoln Hall was open to anyone who would dare live there. Mercifully, the building has since been razed, but at one time Bill Bernard, the vice president for business operations, told me the building was valued at four thousand dollars.

Where God had shut one door, he had opened another. Despite (or because of) the memorable living accommodations in

Lincoln Hall, I developed lifelong friends in ministry and my experience in seminary was a hundred times richer than it would have been living anywhere else.

In hindsight, it became apparent that the possibility of living with my friend was simply something God used to help me overcome my fear of moving to Texas.

This is not unusual. Sometimes the circumstances God uses to guide us change after we have understood God's counsel.

It's Simple to Start

When children are learning to walk, parents do everything in their power to make it as easy as possible. We remove all obstacles from their paths, cheer them incessantly, and usually are right in front of them as they take their first step, trying to motivate them to move forward. This is perfectly natural.

What would be unusual, however, is if I were to do these same things with my six-year-old daughter who has been walking for five years! She does not need me to make it that simple for her to walk. Instead, my wife and I transferred those tangible incentives to helping her learn to use the potty, then ride a bike, and then go off to school.

As God teaches us to follow his leading and recognize his voice, he works with us as a parent works with a child. When a person first begins to look to God for guidance, God is there like a parent helping a toddler walk. His response can often come quickly and in very tangible ways. As we grow in our ability to hear God's voice, he wants to stretch our faith so that we can experience more of the rich depth of his voice. There are times when he might require more earnest effort, more prayer, and more waiting than we have ever done before. Sometimes he may even require us to rely on others to help us seek his voice, since God is constantly moving us toward recognizing the value and importance of community.

For those who are just beginning to listen to God's voice, this is good news. God wants you to be successful in hearing his voice.

Many of the details of the stories here will not be required of you, at least not the first few times you listen for God's voice.

Please Confirm

Experience has taught me that God understands what a struggle it can be to hear his voice. That is why he gradually eases us into it. This is also why he seems not to mind when we ask him for confirmation that we have truly understood his guidance—especially when his leading seems counterintuitive.

Take the example of David in 1 Samuel 23. David was on the run from Saul. Six hundred distressed and discontented Israelites joined him, and David became the leader of a small fighting force, running for their lives from Saul. One day, David got word that Philistines were attacking the Israelite city of Keilah. The Bible says that David inquired of God, "should I attack Keilah?" God clearly tells him that he should go and attack the Philistines and save Keilah.

Full of idealistic zeal and energized that he has heard from the Lord, David boldly announced to his group that they would be attacking the Philistines and saving Keilah. No sooner have the words left his mouth than the grumbling began. "If we are terrified living in Judah, how much worse is it going to be if we actually attack the Philistines!" To a man, they all agreed this was a crazy plan. Shaken in his confidence, David went back to the Lord and asked again. Maybe he misheard. Maybe it was all a dream. Again God tells him to go and attack Keilah, but this time he adds the reassuring words, "I will give them into your hands" (see v. 4).

God never got mad at David for asking the same question again just to confirm his answer was from the Lord. God knows doubts have sprung up in David's mind because his men think this is such a ludicrous idea. After all, it is a ludicrous idea! So God graciously offers confirmation. He does the same for Gideon, giving him multiple signs and confirmations in Judges 6 as Gideon tries to come to grips with the crazy assignment God has given him.

There are times when we need to go back to God for confirmation about his guidance. Perhaps it is because of a lack of faith. More likely it is the natural consequence of major dissuasions, changing circumstances, or the radical nature of what God is calling us to do. The more difficult the path, the more confirmation we need. I have always found God to be gracious and understanding—and willing to provide the confirmation.

Still Plagued by Doubts

You would think that after all these years of listening to God's voice, I would no longer doubt God's ability and willingness to communicate with me. But, unfortunately, I am still plagued by the same old doubts. Although God has answered my inquiries countless times, I often find myself in need of hearing from him again and thinking, *This time he won't answer*, or, *This time he'll miss the deadline.*

God is never predictable. After all, God once communicated his guidance to Gideon by having him eavesdrop as others discussed their dreams (see Judg. 7:10–14); in another case he talked to Josiah through the Pharaoh of Egypt who was coming to attack him (see 2 Chron. 35:21). You never know how God is going to communicate his guidance. In fact, the personal experiences of Lewis Chafer, the founder of Dallas Seminary, led him to the conclusion that God never seems to guide us in the same way twice.[5] Unfortunately this level of uncertainty can lead to fear and doubt.

For example, three years ago I was on a study break, spending time preparing to preach on the book of Exodus. I was terrified of Exodus, having never preached through an entire Old Testament book before. I happened to take with me volume 1 of John Goldingay's *Old Testament Theology*, thinking that it might be useful. As I read, God began to open up Exodus to me. Through what I was reading, God guided me through the process of laying out the sermon series. It was an incredible experience. Two years later I was due to go on my study break again, this time to prepare material on the Gospel of John. As I indicated in chapter 3, one of the ways God told me to preach on John was that I was given a book on the theology of John as a present. Convinced that God would use this book to open up the riches of John's Gospel the way he had used Goldingay's book, I didn't take any other books on John with me! Yet somewhere in the middle of my study break, it became clear that God was not speaking to me through the book. I began to panic. I became convinced that this time God wouldn't help me—and then what would I do? The doubt was debilitating and quickly turned to anger. Yet God graciously met me in my anger and gave me the guidance I needed with a prompting that came during an anger-laced prayer. Embarrassed by my doubt, I was reminded that God is never predictable, just faithful!

No one ever "arrives" in this journey of being guided by God. I still find it to be a struggle to listen to God's voice, though the struggle manifests itself in different ways than it did years ago. What I have learned is that no matter where you are on the spectrum of hearing from God, he will usually ask you to stretch a little beyond what you think you can do in order to hear from him. In this way, whether we are beginners or veterans in hearing God's voice, we are all in the same boat. Each one of us must walk by faith, trusting in God and encouraging one another to keep believing that God will lead us and guide us.

Discussion Questions

1. Have you experienced any of these same lessons in your life as you listened for guidance from God? What other lessons have you learned in seeking advice from the Lord?

2. One of the most important lessons I have learned is that listening to God does not create a problem-free life. On the other hand, we saw in chapter 2 that listening to God does save us from a host of problems that happen when

we make decisions ourselves. How do you think these two ideas fit together?

3. Another really important lesson for me is recognizing that because God is always stretching me, listening to him will always be something of a struggle. Where are you on this journey? What doubts or struggles are you experiencing as you go through the process of listening for God's guidance?

8

telling others

In this candid confession from the pages of her diary, Hannah Whitall Smith puts to words what many people feel:

> I never want to hear anybody say again, "The Lord led me to do this," or "The Lord led me to do that." Not that I do not believe in His leading, but I am convinced it is more through our judgment and reason than through our emotions that He leads, and such emotional persuasion does not make us infallible.[1]

Very few statements raise such hackles as "God told me." People in my life complain that I use such language too often.

"How can you be sure that you have heard from God?"

"You are just trying to attach God's name to decisions you made on your own!"

"All discussion ends when you say that!"

"What makes you so special that God would talk to you? When you talk this way, it makes me feel like I am missing out on something."

In the face of such criticism, would it not be better to simply keep quiet about God's guidance? After all, using such language can expose a person to ridicule, shut down important dissenting opinions, and cause hard feelings.

Or, despite all this, should we share with others that God has led and guided us? If so, how should we do so?

"It Seemed Good to the Holy Spirit"

It was the first major controversy the church had ever faced. Almost everyone was talking about it. On one side, some Jewish Christians were claiming that Gentile converts needed to be circumcised and obey the Law of Moses. How could anyone be a follower of the Jewish Messiah if they refused to obey Mosaic Law? On the other side, equally vigorous arguments were being shouted back. If Gentile converts had to be circumcised, then Christ died in vain! If Christ set everyone free from the curse of the law, why would anyone need to follow it to become a Christian? This was no small matter.

Needing guidance, they took this matter to the Christian leadership in Jerusalem. If anyone would know the right thing to do, they would. So in Acts 15, the leadership convened the first council in Christian history to discuss the matter. All the major players were there: the pillars of the church Peter, James, and John; the other apostles and elders; the superstar missionary team Paul and Barnabas; and a group of highly vocal, highly influential former Pharisees.

Looking for guidance from God, the council began to sift through the evidence. Peter told about his experience with Cornelius. Paul and Barnabas reported what God's Spirit was doing on the mission field. In both cases God had accepted Gentile believers apart from obedience to the Mosaic Law. James noted that their testimony matched what Amos 9 had predicted. So he announced: "It is my judgment, therefore, that we should not make it difficult for the Gentiles who are turning to God" (Acts 15:19). The council was in agreement.

The really interesting twist comes, however, when the council decides to write a letter explaining their decision to the churches. The letter does not say, "It is our judgment." Instead it says, "It seemed good *to the Holy Spirit* and to us" (v. 28). Wait a minute. At no time does Acts 15 ever say that the Holy Spirit spoke audibly to the apostles and elders during their deliberations. Instead, they followed a process not unlike the one I've described in this book. They looked for God's leading through circumstances and listened to his voice speaking through his Word and in community. From these things they determined that God had led them to this conclusion. And here is the important part for us: they go out of their way to say so! They could easily have said, "it is our judgment," or "we have decided," or "it seemed good to us." By saying, "it seemed good to the Holy Spirit," the leadership is claiming, "God told us."

Now some may argue that these were apostles and elders, and this was a major theological matter, so we can't compare their story to our situation today. But the fact remains that these apostles and elders not only felt as if God spoke through circumstances, his Word, and the council of elders and apostles, but they also explicitly identified this decision as being from the Lord.

To Testify or Not to Testify

The all-encompassing question with regard to whether we share our stories with others is: Has God spoken? Has he provided guidance? Has his voice been heard through signs, wisdom, or through circumstances? If he has, should we not share this with others? I believe there are four reasons it is imperative to do so.

First, it is deceitful to refrain from acknowledging God's guidance. It is true that if God has not spoken, and we say that he has, we are lying. But if God has spoken and we through our silence refuse to acknowledge his leading, this too is a form of deceit. Jesus has commissioned us to be his witnesses (see Acts 1:8). If we are to truly bear witness about Jesus, we must testify to the fact that he is the Good Shepherd who leads and guides his followers. As Ben Campbell Johnson reminds us, "If we are to give worthy testimony to our faith, we must name the interventions and disclosures of God in our lives. . . . Testimony doesn't refer to a general condition, nor does it build on an ambiguous experience of God; it reports definite, specific encounters with God."[2] When God gives us guidance and counsel, we experience definite, specific encounters with him.

Second, if we refuse to acknowledge God's leading, we steal his glory. Earlier I used the example of God the Father guiding Jesus in the choice of the twelve apostles. While it is true that Jesus sometimes says that he chose the Twelve (see John 6:70), he also attributes this choice to the Father (see John 17:6, 9). One of the reasons he tells us the Father led him to choose these twelve men is so that God might receive glory. In fact, Jesus tells us that everything he does is guided by God (see John 5:19; 8:28). Why does he tell us this? So that we will glorify the Father in heaven. That's the goal. When we refuse to acknowledge God's leading, we rob him of glory. After all, if we don't say "God led me," or "I sensed this was from the Lord," then who will get the credit for the decisions when they work out? When we are silent, we lead people to think that we are the masters of our fate and captains of our soul, rather than those who are dependent on the leading of a gracious and kind Father.

True, but don't we open God up to unnecessary criticism when we attach his name to decisions in our lives? What if they don't work out? Aren't we actually contributing to diminishing God's glory? Again, if God has not guided and we say he has, we do damage to his reputation. But God does not need a defense attorney or an image consultant. Nor does he need a publicist trying to protect him from bad press. After all, Moses does not hide the fact that God told him to confront Pharaoh, even though the first time all that resulted was Israel having to make bricks without straw. Moses could have left God out of it until the plagues started. Likewise, Jesus does not hide the fact that the Father chose the Twelve, even though we might have wanted to "protect" God from having chosen Judas Iscariot. Everything God does brings him glory, and when we subjectively pick and choose when and if to acknowledge his leading, we rob him of glory.

Third, when we explicitly acknowledge God's guidance, God can use our testimony to guide others. Donald Barnhouse, a great Christian preacher from the 1900s, tells the story of being in Schenectady, New York, speaking to a group that included many young engineers from General Electric. He reports:

> I spoke of feeding upon Christ, pointing out that the physical action of today was the result of last week's food, and that the spiritual action in any life is the result of previous feeding upon Christ. I said, "For example, a young man trained as an engineer, with bright prospects before him, hears the call of God to go out to Africa as a missionary, leaves his position, and faces the Dark Continent. He has been feeding on Christ." I had no more than pronounced the benediction than a young man came up to me and asked, "Why did you say what you did about an engineer going to Africa?" I answered that, as I was preaching, *the Holy Spirit had led me.* And the young man replied, "I am an engineer and God is calling me to Africa, and I must leave my career and go there as a missionary." It was a "word fitly spoken," which reached his particular case.[3]

What if Barnhouse had said, "I just decided to say it," instead of, "The Holy Spirit led me"? Because Barnhouse was honest and gave credit to the Lord, God was able to speak through that statement to the young man, confirming in his heart that he was indeed calling him to quit his job for the mission field.

Fourth, when we testify that God has guided us, we encourage others to listen for God's voice themselves. If Gideon, Samuel, Nehemiah, and Daniel had not said, "God told me," in so many words, we would have no idea that God speaks in this way to guide people. If Origen, Wesley, Spurgeon, and Darlene Rose had not reported, "God guided me," we would have no confidence that God guides outside the pages of Scripture. If Chad, Toran, Darla, Steve, and Cindy had not told their stories of God's leading, we would have no assurance that God guides ordinary Christians even today.

One of my prayers for this book is that, if nothing else, it begins to raise your expectations that you will hear from God. The point of including stories from the Bible, from history, and from ordinary people is to foster the realization that God does indeed lead and guide. When we speak of his guidance, we encourage others to listen for his voice.

How to Speak of God's Guidance

If, then, we should name the times when God speaks into our lives, how do we go about talking about God's leading and guiding? Here are some guidelines I find helpful.

Be Honest about Your Certainty

In my experiences of hearing from God, there are differing levels of certainty. When I was called to be the senior pastor of Calvary Church, God spoke in so many clear, unambiguous ways to so many people that when I speak of my position I always say, "God called me to be the pastor of this church." There was no doubt in my mind, and there is no doubt in my language.

On the other hand, there have been decisions along the way that I thought were from the Lord, but I was not nearly as certain. In those cases, I tend to use language like, "I sense that this might be from the Lord," "I might be wrong, but my best guess is that God is leading in this way," "I haven't received clear direction, but I do have a sense of peace about this decision," or "I wouldn't say, 'God definitively told me,' but this is where the evidence seems to be pointing."

Now some people, like me, are prone to exaggeration and hyperbole (or should I say some people absolutely exaggerate every single little thing!). We see things more in black and white, but exercising a little restraint in this area goes a long way in protecting against the damage unguarded language can cause.

I remember when my wife told me she was pregnant with our first child. She hung up two banners in our apartment. One said "It's a Boy" and the other "It's a Girl." One day when I came home from class, the "It's a Boy" banner had fallen to the floor and "It's a Girl" remained on the wall. Could this be a sign from God? Weeks later, on our way to an ultrasound, a person who likes to tease me about how I am always "hearing from the Lord" asked tongue-in-cheek if God had told me the gender of our baby. I should have said, "Something happened to give me a hunch that this is a girl." Instead, wanting to validate my position, I confidently stated that God had said it was a girl. This was silly. A banner falling to the floor was no basis for this kind of confident, prophetic statement. When I returned and announced we were having a boy, I was subject to some well-deserved, good-natured ribbing, and we all had a laugh. But I didn't represent God as well as I could have.

For other people who are the masters of understatement, it is important to avoid the opposite danger of taking clear communication from God and presenting it as if God had been unclear. I realize that some will be uncomfortable with the specific words, "God told me." That's just not your personality. That's fine. Find a way to say it that is more comfortable for you. Maybe something like, "I prayed earnestly and this is where I sensed God was guiding me," "All signs from God pointed in this direction," "The fingerprints of God were pretty clear," or "It was of the Lord."

Or perhaps using Nehemiah's language: "God put it in my heart" (Neh. 2:12; 7:5).

The goal in each case is to point people to God, not to ourselves.

Hindsight Is Closer to 20/20

Testimonies narrate what God has done in the past. Being farther away from events allows for more perspective in discerning

God's fingerprints. One of the reasons the Bible is so definitive about God's leading is that those who recorded the events have the benefit of the perspective that distance brings.

This means I am more likely to use confident language about what happened in the past, after sufficient reflection, than what is happening in the present or what I think God is saying about the future. In other words, you would more likely hear me say, "God called me," than "God is calling me." There are still times in the present when it is necessary to name God's intervention as it is happening so that others can see God's leading as well, but it is usually better to speak in the past tense about God's guiding.

I shared that God told me to become an engineer when I was entering college. I can say that with complete confidence now, but if you would have asked me during my freshman year if God was telling me to be an engineer, I would have had nothing more than a faint sense that this was the path God put me on. Only with the benefit of hindsight can I see how God used seeming coincidences to lead me in that direction.

Sometimes a little time will cause us to lower our certainty. There are times I have heard myself utter the phrase, "Well, I thought God was leading us in this direction, but it is not as clear now." Patience in reporting what God has said or done will allow us to testify more accurately about whether or not he has guided.

For this reason, it is good to write down your stories of God's guiding. This allows you to capture the emotions and details both for later reflection and for sharing accurate testimony.

Testimonies Are Usually Personal

Another guiding principle: use much more cautious language when communicating something God might be telling someone else. A few years ago, I was convinced that God was calling a man in our church to serve in a particular volunteer position in the church. When asked, the man felt strongly that this position was not for him. I assumed that this was only because he had not spent time listening to God (a poor assumption on my part). So I told him I was certain God wanted him to do this. This was a mistake. Softer language would have been both kinder and wiser. Although the strength of my language rattled him, he was fortunately not overpowered by it. In light of his resistance, I began to question whether or not I had heard from God, so we agreed to seek God's guidance one more time. As we together inquired of the Lord, God made it clear that I had not understood his leading correctly the first time. Looking back, I wished I had used more subtle language.

It is interesting to note that in the Acts 15 passage discussed above, the apostles and elders worded their letter to the Christian churches in such a way as to say, "It seemed good to the Holy Spirit and to us." They would, of course, have been right to word their letter, "thus says the Lord." Instead, they chose milder language—a helpful principle when we comment on ways God might be guiding others through us.

Others Help Us See More Clearly

When others recognize that God is the one doing the leading, we can become more confident in testifying to his direction in our lives.

A woman was in my office recently who in her early childhood had suffered through some horrible things, which caused her great pain. When she reached her college years, she responded by committing ungodly actions, which only added to the pain. Yet God in his grace reached out to her. Professional counseling helped her deal with issues from her past and she experienced some level of healing. But she was still unable to share with anyone but her husband what she had been through. She was silent because she was afraid of being rejected, even as she continued growing in her faith and serving God. For twenty years she kept the secrets of her past hidden.

One day, however, she found herself in my office at God's prompting. He opened her mouth and she began to share her story with me. Confident that I was going to be horrified, she

175

was dumbfounded when, with tears in my eyes and a smile on my face, I told her, "That's about one of the best stories I have ever heard! No wonder Satan has been trying to keep you from sharing it with anyone else." As we went back through her story, I pointed out the ways that God had been present with her: protecting her, forgiving her, and guiding her. Only with the help of someone else was she able to see that God had not abandoned her. He had always been her Good Shepherd, leading her through life. Now he was leading her to the point of testifying to others. Instead of being confused as to what God was doing, she could now see his involvement crystal clearly. Instead of refusing to even speak of it, she has begun to share with others how God rescued her and how he is actively guiding her.

Ending the Discussion?

A final guiding principle is this: if we are truly looking for the leading of God, then we must be careful not to allow our language to cut off dialogue with others who can help us find or confirm God's leading.

When we assert confidently that we have already heard from God, it can kill a discussion with all but the stoutest of dialogue partners. After all, what is left to say after someone says, "but God told me"?

Yet there is a tension here. If we are to truly dialogue with others in searching for God's guidance, we have to share what we think God is telling us and why we think it. It makes no sense trying to pretend that we are transferring jobs because it is the wise thing to do when the only reason is that God keeps pressing on our hearts to do so. Wisdom is required to effectively name God's working without silencing others.

And what if we find ourselves in the opposite position: not the one looking for God's leading but the concerned friend who hears "God told me," even though the evidence doesn't seem to point in that direction?

We must remember that even if someone claims to have heard from God, we have a responsibility to share our honest opinion if given the opportunity to do so. Who knows? God may use our resistance to rescue someone from mishearing his guidance. Or he may use our resistance to provide additional confirmation of his leading, as happened to me a number of years ago.

In 2001, Lisa and I felt strongly that God was calling us overseas so that I could work on a PhD. God had not only planted this desire in our hearts, he had opened the doors both financially and academically in jaw-dropping ways. Yet I knew my dad would not like the idea. So while I told God I would follow his leading no matter what, I began to pray he would cause my dad to be open to it.

The day came to sit down with my parents. I told them I felt God was leading us to quit our jobs, sell our possessions, and move overseas. My confidence that this was from God did not automatically persuade my dad, so he began to ask questions. He asked if I was planning for a career in academia, for which a PhD would be a requirement. "No," I replied.

"What kind of job are you interested in?"

I described for him my ideal job.

"Isn't that the exact job you have now?"

Sheepishly, I admitted it was.

"So you want to leave your job, go spend a lot of time and money trying to get a degree, only so you can hopefully get the same type of job when you are done?"

It did sound pretty foolish when he said it. It looked like God had not answered my prayers about changing my dad's heart.

But at that moment, God placed a thought in my head that I had never before in my life considered. It came so completely out of the blue that it struck even me by surprise.

"When I was sick and almost died (at age two), did you ever promise God that if he healed me, he could do anything he wanted with me?"

"No."

The answer was immediate and resounding. But it was my mom's voice that had spoken. My dad was strangely silent. Tears started to form in his eyes. After a minute he said quietly, "I did."

Everyone in the room was startled—my mom and I because we had never heard this before; my dad because for twenty-nine years he had never told a living soul. Into the silence I said, "I think God is asking you to let us go do this with your blessing." My dad agreed.

If my dad had simply rolled over when I said, "but I think this is from the Lord," we both would have missed out on this blessing. I received an additional confirmation that God was calling us to go do this schooling, and my dad received grace to know firsthand that this was from the Lord.

Conclusion

How we speak about God's leading and guiding is incredibly important. We must be careful not to overstate or understate our certainty; we should recognize the value that a little hindsight can bring to accurately represent what God has said; we should be especially careful when telling others what God might be saying to us about them; and we should allow others to help us see more clearly God's leading in our lives, so that we can testify as truthfully as possible. It can be tough to navigate through these complexities. I have made many mistakes in this area. Yet despite the difficulties we must surely tell others when God provides us with counsel and advice, guiding us through life. We want to be like hymn writer Fanny Crosby, who testified:

> All the way my Savior leads me,
> What have I to ask beside?
> Can I doubt His tender mercy,
> Who through life has been my Guide?
> Heav'nly peace, divinest comfort,
> Here by faith in Him to dwell!
> For I know, whate'er befall me,
> Jesus doeth all things well;
> For I know, whate'er befall me,
> Jesus doeth all things well.

All the way my Savior leads me,
Cheers each winding path I tread,
Gives me grace for every trial,
Feeds me with the living Bread.
Though my weary steps may falter
And my soul athirst may be,
Gushing from the Rock before me,
Lo! A spring of joy I see;
Gushing from the Rock before me,
Lo! A spring of joy I see.

All the way my Savior leads me,
Oh, the fullness of His love!
Perfect rest to me is promised
In my Father's house above.
When my spirit, clothed immortal,
Wings its flight to realms of day
This my song through endless ages:
Jesus led me all the way;
This my song through endless ages:
Jesus led me all the way.

Discussion Questions

1. In this chapter I offer different examples you can use to talk to someone about God's leading. What different ways of saying "God told me" are you most comfortable with and why?

2. Some people need to be more bold in speaking out about God's leading, and others need to be more reserved in how they speak about his guidance. Where are you on that spectrum? What steps can you take to help improve in this area?

3. Have you ever shared with another person how God led you? How did you do it? What was their response?

conclusion

In **Lewis Carroll's** brilliantly creative classic, *Alice in Wonderland*, Alice comes one day to a fork in the road and sees the Cheshire Cat in a tree.

> "Which road do I take?" she asked.
> "Where do you want to go?" he responded.
> "I don't know," Alice answered.
> "Then," said the cat, "it doesn't matter."[1]

Compare the Cheshire Cat's attitude with David's portrayal of God in Psalm 23: "The LORD is my shepherd, I lack nothing. He makes me lie down in green pastures, he leads me beside quiet waters, he refreshes my soul. He guides me along the right paths for his name's sake" (vv. 1–3).

The contrast could not be greater. Lewis Carroll's Cheshire Cat cares nothing for poor, lost Alice. He offers no help and no guidance. He is a grinning, disappearing enigma. God, on the other hand, presents himself as our Good Shepherd who loves us totally and completely. He leads and guides us down pathways to still waters and green pastures even when we have no idea where we want to or should go.

Perhaps I find the contrast between the Cheshire Cat's response and God's self-testimony so striking because I remember standing in the gardens of Christ Church in Oxford, England, looking at the tree where a cat once perched and inspired Lewis Carroll. I was in that garden because God had clearly and powerfully guided me down a path that led me to be a student in that place.

After God told us we were to go to Oxford, Lisa and I began to wonder how in the world we would pay for something like that. After looking through our finances, we decided that if this was what God was calling us to do, we needed to sell all our possessions to fund this adventure. We were overly optimistic about our abilities to pay, but one Saturday, sitting in our apartment, we made the decision to liquidate everything. It turned out not to be necessary. Just two days later, we received a phone call from some dear friends whom we hadn't seen in quite a while. They informed us that God had been telling them they needed to help us financially with whatever we were being called to do next in life. Our friends were calling to find out what God was leading us to do. Dumbfounded, I told them he was sending us overseas. They asked how much it would cost. I reluctantly told them, convinced that once they comprehended the shocking number, they would be sure they had misheard God. Instead, they asked if they could pay for the whole thing: moving expenses, tuition, room and board, plus spending money—for three years!

One of the great reasons for listening to God's voice is that he can make happen whatever it is he guides us to do. In this case he had spoken not only to us, but also to our friends, encouraging them to provide financially for our needs.

One of the greatest experiences of my life has been regularly hearing the voice of God lead and direct me. If nothing else, my prayer for this book is that it will raise your expectations regarding God communicating with you. The pages of Scripture are filled with examples of those who received guidance and direction from God. These can't be isolated examples for select individuals. There are simply too many examples, from all over the Bible, featuring every different kind of person. And these are only the ones actually written down! Why would God have recorded so many examples if not to convince us that he is the God who guides?

Likewise, the pages of history are littered with many hundreds of thousands of examples of God speaking. What are we to make of people such as Origen, Polycarp, Augustine, Francis of Assisi, Ignatius of Loyola, John Wesley, Charles Spurgeon, Elisabeth Elliot, Billy Graham, Bill Hybels, and so many, many more who heard the voice of God guiding them and directing them? Today, God is no less communicative than he was in the past. His counsel has never been limited to a select few or to unique circumstances. It is part and parcel with what it means for him to be our Father.[2] It is part of Jesus's role as Counselor, Prophet, Priest, Shepherd, and Spouse.[3] True, God rarely force-feeds counsel to those who refuse to listen, but if God doesn't play favorites, surely we can conclude that his guidance is not for just a select few. So my hope and prayer are that you will have a greater longing to hear his voice and willingness to listen for his leading and direction.

Yet, I must warn you one last time: the process of hearing from God can be frustrating, because he is in control and we are not. But the way I see it, we have a choice: make decisions ourselves using human wisdom alone, or wait for God to guide us. Both ways involve a certain amount of stress. Making decisions without consulting God is often easier and more controllable, but it can lead to far greater struggles, angst, and stress after the decision is made. We often end up second-guessing our decision because our choice resulted in unexpected and unintended consequences, or we end up with the nagging feeling that we have settled for a safe, "wise" path instead of the adventures only God could dream up for us. I have made decisions both ways. In my experience, I prefer the wrestling and confusion before a decision rather than after.

So now it is time for you to begin. Or begin again.

Reading a book like this is just the start of a journey. I can do no better than to point you in God's direction and say, "listen." Each one of Jesus's sheep must learn to recognize his voice for themselves. Eli couldn't listen for Samuel, and I cannot listen for you. But if you are willing to listen, God will speak. He will give you guidance, direction, counsel, and advice for whatever situation you need his help for, or whatever phase of life you find yourself in.

It all starts with a simple prayer: "Speak, Lord, your servant is listening." Prepare your heart to receive guidance from God. Ask yourself the five questions from chapter five:

Are you pure in God's eyes?

Are you willing to do whatever God advises?

Are you willing to abandon all other means of making these decisions?

Are you willing to wrestle with and wait for God?

Do you believe God is a good communicator?

If so, then begin to ask God for counsel and advice. Set aside time to fast, pray, and be alone with God. Read through the Scriptures. Seek godly counsel. Participate in your local church. Look for the fingerprints of God. Take note of what is happening in your life. Open your ears and listen to what God might be saying to you.

For what the psalmist declares is still true today: "Yet, I am always with you; you hold me by my right hand. You guide me with your counsel, and afterward you will take me into glory" (Ps. 73:23–24).

Discussion Questions

1. Is there anything still hindering you from seeking guidance from the Lord?

2. Who is someone you know who could help you listen for guidance from God?

3. What decision are you currently facing for which you would most like God to provide counsel?

frequently asked questions

How does what you are talking about relate to "God's will"?

Traditionally, the subject of God's leading and guiding is addressed using the language of "God's will for our lives." While the Bible does use this terminology at times to address these issues, the biblical use of "God's will" entails more than just personal guidance.[1] For this reason, I find the language of "God's will" as it is used today to be unhelpful and confusing. To speak of God's will places what we have been talking about here in the realm of morality and sin. From such a point of view, God's will is something that we obey or disobey, just like the commandments from God given in the pages of Scripture. This raises questions such as, "If it is a sin to disobey God's will, does this mean it has the same authoritative status as Scripture?", "Am I in the center of God's will?", and "Are those who fail to find out God's will also sinning?" Such questions orient the discussion in the wrong direction.

To speak of God's will also places the discussion in the realm of predestination. From such a point of view, we are to discover God's predetermined will for our lives. This raises philosophical questions such as, "Does God have a specific will for every

possible decision of our lives?" and "Does one person's disobedience frustrate God's plan?" Again, I don't find such discussions
to be helpful.

What is more fruitful for me is to think about the guidance
and leading of God under the rubric of counsel, advice, and
wisdom. Guidance from God is less about right and wrong,
and more about better and worse. In other words, it fits more
closely with Proverbs than it does with Leviticus. It fits more
naturally with God as Shepherd than with God as Judge. God
is, of course, both Judge and Shepherd, just like Proverbs and
Leviticus are both part of God's Word. But different books and
different descriptions of God help us to approach the magnitude
of God's glory in different ways.

What I mean is that guidance from God is more like wisdom
from God and less like laws from God. After all, the decision of
the new college graduate to become an accountant rather than
a salesman is not a decision about what is right or wrong. It is a
decision about what is better or worse. Rather than thinking about
discovering God's will for your life, I am talking about receiving
advice and counsel from God on what is the best choice to make.
If you graduate from college and decide you do not need God's
advice on what career to embark on, so be it. I think it would be
foolish to not seek counsel from God—not because you would be
in danger of sinning if you chose to be an accountant, but because
being an accountant might not be the best career for you as you
seek to participate in what God wants to do in and through you.

For this reason I do not spend time in this book discussing passages such as Acts 18:21; 21:14; 1 Corinthians 4:19; 16:7; or James
4:13–17, which discuss travel plans in light of "God's will." Nor
do I discuss passages such as 1 Corinthians 1:1, which speaks of
Paul being called to be an apostle by the will of God, or Galatians
2:7–9, which talks about God calling Paul to be an apostle to the
Gentiles. There is obviously some level of "guidance" included in
such calls. But something else seems to be involved here as well.
Paul's calling to be an apostle strikes me as different than God
guiding him to stay in Corinth for an extended period of time.

This book is addressing issues that are often labeled "God's will," but the language and approach presented here is somewhat different.

Isn't the notion of guidance from God ripe for abuse?

Isn't what I am proposing here ripe for abuse? Wouldn't it be much safer to limit ourselves to input from God that is found only in the pages of Scripture? Indeed, I could fill an entire book with the ways in which people have abused the idea of God's guidance. A prophet lied to the man of God in 1 Kings 13, claiming "God told me." Shemaiah was hired to lie to Nehemiah about God's guidance (see Neh. 6:10–13). Single men have used "God told me to go out with you" as a pick-up line. Christians have rationalized decisions to pursue unbiblical divorces as being guidance from God. Power-hungry autocrats have stifled all disagreement with claims of having heard from God. What about Oral Roberts's celebrated statement in 1987 that God told him he would take him to heaven if he didn't raise $8 million? The list could go on and on.

Why not pursue the strategy that Haddon Robinson suggests in *Decision Making by the Book*: "When we find ourselves facing tough choices in life—those day-in, day-out decisions which make up the very fabric of our existence—we shouldn't seek special messages from God. Instead we should ask, 'How do we develop the skills necessary to make wise and prudent choices.'"[2] Such an approach seems much safer.

The problem is that every form of communication from God is open to distortion by fallen humans. When God gave Adam and Eve explicit instructions in the Garden, Satan twisted and perverted them (see Gen. 3:1). The words that Jesus spoke, as the Word of God, were taken and twisted to serve selfish human means (see Mark 14:58). The Bible can be twisted, misinterpreted, and abused (see Matt. 4:6).

Perhaps the closest analogy to abusing guidance from God is the unfortunate fact of false prophets. False prophets have been a plague on the people of God from the beginning of the Bible through the last pages of Revelation. But God does not stop speaking through prophets simply because prophecy is open to abuse. So it is with his guidance. Yes, there are people running around falsely claiming to have received guidance from God, but God is not forced into silence because of their abuse. We must not throw the baby out with the bathwater.

Does God always answer?

Chapter 5 discussed some prerequisites to hearing advice from God: purity, willingness to wait for and wrestle with God, abandoning plan B, willingness to do whatever God says, and believing that God is a good communicator. But what if you have done or are doing all of these to the most reasonable degree possible—is there ever a time when God will refuse to give you the guidance that you seek?

I should admit upfront that there is a tension here between what the Bible seems to imply and the experiences of many Christians. The Bible seems to imply that everyone who seeks guidance will receive it. James 1:5 says, "*If any of you* lacks wisdom, you should ask God, who gives generously to all without finding fault, *and it will be given to you*" (emphasis mine). In general, the passages on prayer in the Bible, under which asking for guidance is a subset, also seem to imply that everyone who asks will receive. Matthew 7:7–11 says,

> Ask and it will be given to you; seek and you will find; knock and the door will be opened to you. For everyone who asks receives; the one who seeks finds; and to the one who knocks, the door will be opened. Which of you, if his son asks for bread, will give him a stone? Or if he asks for a fish, will give him a snake? If you then, though you are evil, know how to give good gifts to your children, how much more will your Father in heaven give good gifts to those who ask him!

If we are longing for guidance and advice from God, is there any indication from these passages that we won't receive it? Likewise, when we look at narrative stories throughout the Bible where people are asking for guidance from God, they all receive this advice, except in those cases where one of the aforementioned prerequisites was missing. In fact, in most biblical narratives the fact that God will respond is a foregone conclusion. For example, when Rebekah wanted to know why her twins were jostling within her, the text simply says she went to inquire of the Lord. The very next words of the text are, "the Lord said to her" (see Gen. 25:22–23). This pattern is repeated throughout Scripture. The testimony of Scripture is that when we ask for guidance, God will answer.

However, balanced against the testimony of Scripture is a large volume of anecdotal personal testimony where people tell us that they have asked God for guidance and he was silent. I am not in a position to know in these cases whether there was sin, a lack of faith in God's ability and willingness to communicate, improper motives, a failure to wrestle or wait for God, or if they abandoned listening to God too soon.

I also cannot know in each of those cases whether God did answer and they failed to recognize his voice. This does happen. For example, my brother-in-law fasted, prayed, and begged God for guidance about whether he should keep doing his business or shut it down and move to another city to pursue work there. During that time, he claimed that God was not answering his requests for guidance. Yet during those months of seeming silence, his business picked up some new clients, the job he was considering in New Mexico failed to materialize, and he got a new roommate and living situation that were a huge blessing to him. As we talked it through, it was clear that God had indeed answered his requests, albeit subtly. Once his eyes were opened, my brother-in-law realized God had responded.

Still, what do we do with the claims of many that they have asked God for guidance and he has not responded? My own response is similar to that of the psalmist in Psalm 37:25 when he says, in a statement that is even more difficult to square with many people's perception of reality: "I was young and now I am old, yet I have never seen the righteous forsaken or their children begging bread." I may not be as old as the psalmist, but for twenty years I have been diligently seeking God's voice in guidance and helping others listen for God's voice. I do admit that there were periods of time during which, if you had asked me, I would have said God doesn't always answer. Likewise there were probably periods of the psalmist's experience during which it seemed as if the righteous had been forsaken. But in the larger picture, when all the evidence is considered—no, the righteous are never forsaken. So it is with guidance from God. After twenty years of observation, my contention is that although there are periods of silence, with much waiting and struggling, God always responds. Like the psalmist, I am convinced that in the end, when everything is said and done, the Bible's witness will prove to be correct and God will be shown to be one who always answers our prayers for guidance.

Can seeking God's guidance be immobilizing?

The number of choices that any one person faces in a single day is innumerable. What to wear to school, what to eat for breakfast, which route to take to work, which friends to engage in conversation . . . and many, many more. If someone tried to fast and pray, read Scripture, examine circumstances, put out fleeces, and wait to hear from the Lord for all these decisions, they would be immobilized, unable to even get out of bed in the morning. Skeptics have used the silliness of such a possibility to dismiss the fact that God guides today as he did in the Scriptures. Yet this hypothetical situation of a believer afraid to get out of bed raises a real danger. It is possible to become immobilized as we look for guidance from God in every situation and for every decision.

Three things are worth noting. First, it is helpful for me to remember that God's guidance is always available, but not always necessary to the same extent. In other words, if on any "minor" decision I need advice, I can ask God for it, but most daily decisions do not require such advice. Does this mean we should only ask God's advice about major decisions like whom to marry?

No. I have asked God for guidance before on what to wear for a given day, or whether or not to speak up in the middle of a conversation. Usually there was something that prompted me to feel as if I needed guidance in that area. Perhaps I was headed to a job interview and wasn't sure what was proper attire, or I was speaking to someone about a particularly sensitive topic and wasn't sure whether or not to mention a piece of information. This seems to be what Nehemiah is doing in Nehemiah 2:4–5 when the king asks him "what do you want?" Nehemiah notes, "Then I prayed to the God of heaven, and I answered the king." It's not hard to imagine that Nehemiah was praying for wisdom and guidance before he spoke, wanting God to lead him into the right words to say. I can't imagine Nehemiah prayed that way before every statement he uttered, but given the situation Nehemiah felt as if he needed guidance from God.

This leads to the second point to keep in mind. The time and effort that I put into seeking guidance from God usually correspond to the magnitude of the decision. If I am wondering what might be the best outfit to wear for a job interview, I may utter a quick, silent prayer and then ask my wife what she thinks, and see if God might not provide some guidance through her. When I am in a conversation with someone and am wondering whether or not to bring something up, I might ask God to lead the conversation in that direction if I am to speak up. On the other hand, if I am wondering whether to hire a person for a specific job, I would spend more time and effort trying to hear God's voice.

Finally, there are some decisions that I am generally seeking guidance from God on, but am mostly waiting for some sort of response. For example, every year I go on a study break. Sometime during the year, I begin to ask God where I should spend that time. Most days this is not very high up on my list of things that I am praying for. In fact, many days I do not pray about it at all. It is a decision that I have asked God for guidance on, and I am waiting for him to reply. As the time for a decision draws nearer, I may increase my prayers about this.

Or as evidence appears, I may begin to ask God more pointedly whether or not he is speaking. For example, this year my cousin announced that she is getting married in Chicago during my study break. Although I had not prayed fervently to that point about the decision, when I heard that news I stopped and asked God if this was his way of leading me to take my study break in Chicago. I took it that it was, and began to make plans accordingly. But the decision about where to take my study break is not a decision I am constantly stressing about so that I am immobilized regarding it.

Why don't we hear the audible voice of God?

Earlier in the book, I stated that we don't normally hear the audible voice of God. Why is that? To begin with, I am not sure that God's audible voice was all that common during Bible times either. Certainly there are times when God spoke audibly, such as at Mt. Sinai in Exodus 20, at Jesus's baptism in Matthew 3, or in response to Jesus's prayer in John 12. And obviously every time Jesus spoke audibly while he was on the earth, God was speaking audibly to people. But we have no indication that when Paul says in Acts 20:23, "the Holy Spirit warns me that prison and hardships are facing me" he has heard an audible voice from heaven. My assumption had always been that when the Bible says such things it is talking about audible voices, but there is no reason why it has to be. In fact, in places like 1 Samuel 16, it seems contextually impossible that God would be using an audible voice.

What appears more likely to me now is that in many cases God was not speaking audibly. His audible voice was so exceptional that the Bible is compelled to note when it happens as in the passages like Exodus 20, Matthew 3, and John 12 mentioned above.

In addition, the New Testament tells us that because of the gift of the Spirit, God's more normal method of communication to us now is internally. God's Spirit speaks to our spirit (see Rom. 8:16; 1 Cor. 2:13) because God dwells within us by his Spirit. If God is unable to speak to our spirit from within, but instead is forced to speak to us from outside ourselves, that is, through our ears, it probably means something is wrong. Therefore, while some non-Christians may hear God's audible voice calling them to salvation, Christians should not expect God to communicate audibly with us.

Of course, when the Spirit is speaking through another person to us we will hear an audible voice, and in that sense we can say we heard God speaking aloud through our friend.

Aren't the narrative stories about God guiding in the Bible descriptive, not prescriptive?

This is an issue raised in chapter 1. While it is true that applying narrative portions of Scripture to our lives today can be trickier than straightforward commands, to say that something is "descriptive" does not nullify its power to command behavior. After all, when my wife says to me, "the trash is full," this is technically a descriptive statement. However, Lisa is not simply informing me of the state of the trash can. She wants me to do something about it.

More importantly, Jesus's attitude toward the narrative portions of the Old Testament is not that they were merely descriptive. When the Pharisees accused Jesus's disciples of breaking the Sabbath by picking grain, Jesus appeals to the story of David eating consecrated bread (see Mark 2:23–27). This story is not merely "descriptive." Jesus sees it as prescribing proper behavior for his disciples.[3]

When God describes how Isaac and Rebekah were married, he is not merely describing to us what happened to satisfy our curiosity for trivia. He wants us to see that the selection of a marriage partner is one opportunity that we have to trust not in our own understanding, but to depend on God. That is why 2 Timothy 3:16–17 says that "All Scripture is God-breathed and is useful for teaching, rebuking, correcting and training in righteousness, so that the servant of God may be thoroughly equipped for every good work." To learn how to live well, we do not look simply to the epistles or the sermons of Jesus. We look to the narrative portions of Scripture as well.[4] And these narrative portions of Scripture point overwhelmingly toward God guiding and directing our lives.

But we understand that it can be difficult to discern exactly what principles some narrative portions of Scripture are attempting to teach us. When we read that Jephthah made a vow that led to him sacrificing his daughter (see Judg. 11:28–40), we are dismayed at his decision and not eager to follow in his footsteps. How then do we know if the stories about God guiding and directing are trying to teach us to do the same today?

Gordon Wenham has recently provided an answer with regard to the Old Testament, arguing that living properly in the Old Testament included much more than simply obeying the law. For example, the rules about marriage in the Bible establish the floor, not the ceiling, of the Bible's teaching about marriage. It is true that all one *has to do* is obey these rules; however, that is not all one *can or should do*. The Scriptures present a much more God-honoring way of finding a spouse than simply checking off obedience to all the rules. Abraham's servant choosing Rebekah is a story that teaches us the virtue of depending on God for such decisions. This principle goes above and beyond what is actually commanded by law, showing us what God desires us to aspire to when making important decisions.

Wenham also offers three commonsense suggestions for how we can know if the stories in the Bible are modeling behavior that should be imitated, as in the case of Isaac and Rebekah as opposed to the case of Jephthah. (1) The behavior pattern should be repeated in a number of different contexts, (2) the behavior should be exhibited in a positive context, and (3) there should be some level of support in the psalms, wisdom books, and other sections of Scripture.[5]

Using these criteria, it is clear that stories involving God guiding and directing should be viewed as part of what we are to do today. First, such stories are found throughout the Scriptures. Second, the stories are always positive—no one is rebuked for inquiring of the Lord, or chastised for failing to have enough

"wisdom" to figure out the answer without God. It is sometimes thought that Gideon should not have needed a fleece from
the Lord, or that Peter should not have cast lots for the twelfth
apostle, but both stories are presented by their authors in a very
positive light. Finally, God as Guide is a theme throughout the
Scriptures. Exodus 15:13 says, "In your unfailing love you will
lead the people you have redeemed. In your strength you will
guide them to your holy dwelling." Psalm 23:2–3 says, "He leads
me beside still waters . . . he leads me with faithfulness."[6] Other
psalms say similar things (see Pss. 32:8–9; 73:24). Even more powerfully, we are directly commanded to seek wisdom from God as
we journey through life (see Prov. 19:20–21; Isa. 58:11; James 1:5)
and those who don't are rebuked for not doing so (see 1 Chron.
10:13–14; Isa. 8:19–20; Hosea 8:4). We can be quite confident
that all these stories about people who looked to God to guide
their decisions are stories meant to encourage us to do the same.

What are Urim and Thummim?

In Exodus 28, God commands that Israel, "Also put the Urim
and the Thummim in the breastpiece, so they may be over Aaron's heart whenever he enters the presence of the LORD. Thus
Aaron will always bear the means of making decisions for the
Israelites over his heart before the LORD" (v. 30). While scholars debate exactly what these were, our best guess is that they
were two stones, perhaps one black and one white, used for
determining God's guidance in decisions that had to be made.
We know very little about them and how they worked, but the
only people we know who used them were the priests (see Lev.
8:8; Num. 27:21; Deut. 33:8; Ezra 2:63; Neh. 7:65). Moses, who
was a prophet and not a priest, never used them. As the office
of prophet came to prominence in the Old Testament, the use
of Urim and Thummim disappeared.

The value of them today seems limited to the recognition
that they are yet another piece of evidence that God desires to
guide and direct his people in the decisions of life.

notes

Introduction

1. J. B. Lightfoot, J. R. Harmer, and Michael W. Holmes, eds., "The Martyrdom of Polycarp," *The Apostolic Fathers* (Grand Rapids: Baker, 1992), 231.

2. Augustine, *Confessions*, 8.28–29.

3. R. W. Southern, "From Schools to University," *The History of the University of Oxford*, vol. 1 (Oxford: Oxford University Press, 1984), 24–25.

4. Graham Howes, *The Art of the Sacred: An Introduction to the Aesthetics of Art and Belief* (London: I. B. Tauris, 2007), 128.

5. Charles Spurgeon, *The Soul Winner* (Grand Rapids: Eerdmans, 1963), 289.

6. George Müller, *A Narrative of Some of the Lord's Dealings with George Müller* (London: J. Nisbet & Co, 1865).

7. Edith Schaeffer, *The Tapestry: The Life and Times of Francis and Edith Schaeffer* (Waco: Word, 1981), 59–62.

8. Mrs. Howard Taylor, *Empty Racks and How to Fill Them* (Dallas Theological Seminary, 1932), 17–18.

9. Christian Smith and Melinda Denton, *Soul Searching: The Religious and Spiritual Lives of American Teenagers* (Oxford: Oxford University Press, 2005). Their label for this approach to God is Moralistic Therapeutic Deism.

Chapter 1 What Is Guidance from God?

1. This translation is from H. G. M. Williamson, *Ezra, Nehemiah* (Waco: Word, 1985), 263. Williamson also provides helpful comments on why Nehemiah 2:12 should be translated using a present participle, as I have done in the previous sentence.

2. I. H. Marshall, *The Gospel of Luke* (Grand Rapids: Eerdmans, 1978), 238.

3. The ESV, in my opinion, correctly translates the Greek text of Acts 19:21. Some translations such as the NIV assume that "in the Spirit" refers to the human

spirit (which is possible since Greek does not use capitals the way that English does) and so they translate the phrase "Paul decided." On the exegesis of the passages, see Darrell Bock, *Acts* (Grand Rapids: Baker, 2007), 605.

4. It is also interesting that James chooses this example to convince us to pray for healing. Why not choose one of the many examples of actual prayers for healing that are in the Old Testament? Instead, James has chosen one prayer request that to our knowledge never applied to any other situation (as far as we know, no one has ever prayed for it not to rain for three and a half years) nor to the situation he is talking about. But his point is that God's intervention in our lives is not exceptional or unique. It is part of what it means to be children of God.

5. Gerald L. Sittser, *The Will of God as a Way of Life* (Grand Rapids: Zondervan, 2004), 219.

Chapter 2 Why Listen for Guidance from God?

1. Careful readers of 1 Samuel 28 will note that, in that instance, Saul did try to seek guidance from God, but God wouldn't respond. To Saul's mind, he had no choice but to consult the witch of Endor, whom 1 Chronicles 10:13 references when it says, "he consulted a medium for guidance." It seems unfair that God turned Saul down and then accused him of not seeking guidance from him. The explanation for this apparent problem is that 1 Chronicles is talking about Saul's general pattern of not seeking guidance from God, not 1 Samuel 28 explicitly. 1 Samuel 28 does contain a specific example of Saul's failure, but here the example is not failure to seek guidance from God, but failure to keep the Word of the Lord, since consulting mediums was expressly forbidden in Israel (see Deut. 18:10–11).

2. The immediate context of this passage refers specifically to guidance for enduring trials, but the more general notion is that God loves to provide wisdom and counsel to those who are seeking it. To these specific encouragements we could have added the broader encouragement to "understand the Lord's will" (Eph. 5:17), but since the Lord's will involves God's moral will and his plan for history as well as matters of personal guidance, I have only included explicit exhortations to seek guidance. For more discussion on why I do not use the phrase "God's will" to describe what I am talking about here, see the appendix.

3. Richard H. Thaler and Cass R. Sunstein, *Nudge: Improving Decisions about Health, Wealth and Happiness* (Penguin: New York, 2008), 7. For a helpful list of reasons why we make irrational decisions, see E. D. Smith, M. Piatelli-Palmarini, and A. T. Bahill, "Cognitive biases affect the acceptance of trade-off studies" in T. Kugler, J. C. Smith, T. Connolly, and Y. J. Son, eds., *Decision Modeling and Behavior in Complex and Uncertain Environments* (New York: Springer, 2008), 227–49.

4. Ori Brafman and Rom Brafman, *Sway: The Irresistible Pull of Irrational Behavior* (New York: Broadway, 2008).

5. Dan Ariely, *Predictably Irrational: The Hidden Forces That Shape Our Decisions*, revised edition (New York: Harper, 2009).

6. Shai Danzinger, Jonathan Levav, and Liora Avnaim-Pesso, "Extraneous Factors in Judicial Decisions," *Proceedings of the National Academy of Science*, 2011.

7. "What's Really Behind Home Field Advantage," *Sports Illustrated*, January 17, 2011. Excerpted from Tobias J. Moskowitz and L. Jon Wertheim, *Scorecasting:*

The Hidden Influences Behind How Sports Are Played and Games Are Won (New York: Random House, 2011).

8. C. H. Spurgeon, *Morning and Evening: Daily Readings* complete and unabridged, new modern edition (Peabody, MA: Hendrickson Publishers, 2006).

9. Ariely, *Predictably Irrational*, 52–53.

10. See for example Sheena Iyengar, *The Art of Choosing* (New York: Hachette, 2010), which is a more popular retelling of her research; also Barry Schwartz, *The Paradox of Choice: Why More Is Less* (San Francisco: HarperCollins, 2005).

11. Thaler and Sunstein, *Nudge*, 97.

12. T. S. Eliot, "The Rock," http://www.wisdomportal.com/Technology/TS-Eliot-TheRock.html.

13. "Document: Toyota warned dealers of throttle surging in 2002," http://www.cnn.com/2010/US/03/22/toyota.throttle.warning/index.html.

14. For a more current corroboration, see Malcolm Gladwell's illuminating essay on marketing women's hair coloring products in *What the Dog Saw: And Other Adventures* (New York: Little, Brown and Co., 2009).

15. Daniel Gilbert, *Stumbling on Happiness* (New York: Knopf, 2006).

16. Rick Hampson, "No Fairy Tale for Lottery Winner," *USA Today*, http://www.usatoday.com/news/nation/2004-12-22-lottery-tragedy_x.htm.

17. C. S. Lewis, *The Weight of Glory: And Other Addresses* (New York: Harper, 1949), 26.

18. I have read several books on the topic of decision making that argue Christians should simply use our God-given wisdom to make decisions rather than seeking direct guidance from God as I am proposing here. In two cases, authors began their books with personal stories about how they sought (and received!) guidance from God for a particular decision. Yet because of the difficulty of the process, they concluded there must be an easier way. This set them on the journey to discover an easier method for making decisions. And some days, I don't blame them!

Chapter 3 How Does God Speak to Us?

1. Brother Yun with Paul Hattaway, *The Heavenly Man: The Remarkable True Story of Chinese Christian Brother Yun* (London: Mill Hill, 2002), 55. Brother Yun's story is filled with examples of God speaking through Scripture. I merely selected the first one that appears in the book. For a defense of Brother Yun and his story, see http://www.asiaharvest.org/pages/news050705OpenLetterBrotherYun.html.

2. The question that came was, "Why did God start churches?" In other words, why didn't God start schools or parachurch organizations, or why didn't he just Christianize the synagogue or the family? That is not the kind of question you can try to answer in a secular academic environment, so the question became, "Why did Paul start churches?" The fruit of my work is published in the academic book *Being Conformed to Christ in Community* (London: T&T Clark, 2008), and is the seeds of the much more readable book *The Gift of Church* (Grand Rapids: Zondervan, 2010).

3. Betty Huizenga, *Apples of Gold* (Colorado Springs: Cook, 2000), 7–8.

4. See David Peterson, *The Acts of the Apostles* (Grand Rapids: Eerdmans, 2009), 375.

5. John Polhill, *The New American Commentary Volume 26: Acts* (Nashville: Broadman, 1992), 290.

6. Peterson, *Acts*, 294. Emphasis mine.

7. Charles Spurgeon, *The Soul Winner* (Grand Rapids: Eerdmans, 1963), 289.

8. Other arguments against Acts 1 include those who think that Paul (and not Matthias) was the twelfth apostle, and therefore the casting of lots failed (but if Paul is the twelfth apostle, no one told him or Luke about it!—see 1 Cor. 15:5; Acts 6:2), and those who think that because Matthias was never heard from again he must have been an invalid choice. But we hear very little in Scripture as to what happened to many of those who are part of the Twelve. This does not invalidate Jesus's choice of them.

9. Why then don't we see casting of lots for leaders after Acts 2? In Acts 1 the apostles are choosing someone for the highest level of authority in the church—someone whose authority would be equal to their own. If they appointed the person, that apostle would be under the authority of the other eleven. After Acts 2 such a scenario does not present itself again. Subsequent selections of leaders happen under the authority of the apostles or established church leaders (see Acts 6; 14:23, Titus 1:5). God is speaking through and supporting the authority structures he put in place.

10. John Piper explains this process in response to the question "What do you think of using casting lots to determine God's will?" http://www.youtube.com/watch?v=YuD8wjDQP44. Video © 2008 by Desiring God Ministries.

11. Susan Damon, "Casting Lots," *Reformed Worship*, March 2008.

12. 2 Kings 20:8–13 and Isaiah 7:1–14, though not exactly the same, both involve God using signs to communicate his guidance and direction.

13. Schaeffer, *Tapestry*, 60–62. Ironically, in her telling of the story Edith Schaeffer argues that Francis would want to discourage others from following his example, but Francis's story is a great illustration for today of asking God to do something extraordinary to confirm the direction he was sensing God leading him.

14. Mark Moring, "Why This 'Secret Millionaire' Went Public," http://www.christianitytoday.com/ct/movies/interviews/2011/secretmillionpublic.html.

15. Taylor, *Empty Racks*, 17–18.

16. Richard Foster, *Celebration of Discipline: The Path to Spiritual Growth* (San Francisco: HarperCollins, 1978), 180.

17. Personal email correspondence, July 2011.

18. James Fenhagen, *More than Wanderers: Spiritual Discipline for Christian Ministry* (New York: Seabury Press, 1981), 35.

19. Ben Campbell Johnson, *The God Who Speaks: Learning the Language of God* (Grand Rapids: Eerdmans, 2004), 122.

20. Megan recorded the longer version of the conversation on her blog *This Is Me Being Real*, http://meganvos.blogspot.com/2010/08/dixie.html.

21. Lindsey's story can be found in *First Person: God in the lives of Oxford Christians*, Anne Keene, Paul Clifford, and Vivienne Larminie, eds., (Oxford: St. Andrews Church, 2005), 27–28.

22. Personal email correspondence, July 2011.

23. G. K. Chesterton, *St. Francis of Assisi* (London: Continuum, 2001), 55–57.

24. David Platt, *Radical* (Colorado Springs: Multnomah, 2010), 174.

Chapter 4 How Do We Distinguish God's Voice?

1. D. A. Carson, *John* (Grand Rapids: Eerdmans, 1991), 383.
2. H. V. Morton, *In the Steps of the Master* (New York: Dodd, Mead and Co., 1937), 180.
3. Daniel Levitin, *This Is Your Brain on Music* (New York: Penguin, 2006), 138–39.
4. Richard Stearns, *The Hole in Our Gospel* (Nashville: Thomas Nelson, 2009), 9.
5. For this reason, it is helpful for me to supplement this image of the Bible as Rosetta Stone with an image that Kevin J. Vanhoozer has developed in *The Drama of Doctrine* (Philadelphia: Westminster John Knox, 2005). Using the image of the theater, Kevin argues that if God is the director/author of the play of history and we are the actors, then the Bible is the script. The script norms the actors' actions and helps them to hear what God is saying. God's interaction with us is not limited to the Bible, but in and through the Bible we come to know our communicative God so that we might recognize the director's direction outside of the script of the Bible. Yet any direction from God is going to be aligned with the script that God himself has written and is using to produce the play of history. See especially chapter 4.
6. "Strictly speaking, 'revelation' does not exhaust the meaning of 'God saying'. The divine discourse encompasses more than disclosing previously unknown information." Vanhoozer, *Drama of Doctrine*, 147.
7. Platt, *Radical*, 164–65.
8. Darlene Deibler Rose, *Evidence Not Seen: A Woman's Miraculous Faith in the Jungles of World War II* (San Francisco: HarperCollins, 1988), 41. This story actually illustrates both the previous point and the current point. Dr. Jaffray's comments about God's guidance supporting the bond of marriage between husband and wife is another example of what I mean when I say that God's guidance supports the structures he has put into place.
9. Ibid. This book is my wife's favorite missionary biography and she highly recommends it for every Christian to read!
10. David G. Brenner, *Desiring God's Will: Aligning Our Hearts with the Heart of God* (Downers Grove, IL: InterVarsity, 2005), 104.
11. Augustine urges a similar principle in the interpretation of Scripture: "All correct interpretations of Scripture must lead us to love God and neighbors above ourselves." *On Christian Doctrine*, book 3, chapter 10. The same is true for recognizing God's voice in daily guidance: any promptings that lead us to love God and others are recognizable as being from the Lord.
12. James Dobson, *Bringing Up Boys* (Wheaton, IL: Tyndale, 2005).
13. Personal email correspondence, July 2011.
14. We do have to acknowledge that many people use their positions of authority for evil and not good. While we need to be careful not to simply ignore advice from people in authority whom we do not like, God's Word always supersedes all other claims of communication from God. This is a complicated topic that is quite situation-specific, but in general, unless the counsel goes against God's Word, God's guidance will support the institutions he has created.
15. What then are we to make of passages such as 1 Kings 22, where God seems to send a lying spirit in order to deceive Ahab? The classic answer to problem

texts such as this is that God allows such spirits to work, rather than commands them to deceive. While God uses deception for his own ends, he does not speak with a voice of deception.

16. Personal email correspondence, July 2011.

17. C. S. Lewis, *The Chronicles of Narnia* (New York: HarperCollins, 1961), 132.

Chapter 5 Preparing to Listen

1. Oswald Chambers, *My Utmost for His Highest*, February 28.

2. See Donald J. Wiseman, *1 & 2 Kings: An Introduction and Commentary* (Downers Grove, IL: InterVarsity, 1993), 186.

3. Lewis Sperry Chafer, *He That Is Spiritual* (Grand Rapids: Zondervan, 1918), 92.

4. This insight is drawn from Dietrich Bonhoeffer, *Sanctorum Communio: A Theological Study of the Sociology of the Church* (Minneapolis: Fortress Press, 1998), 86.

5. John Stott, *Between Two Worlds* (Grand Rapids: Eerdmans, 1982), 94.

6. Goethe, *The Natural Daughter*, Act 5, Scene 7. The translation from the German is from Gerhard von Rad, *Wisdom in Ancient Israel* (Harrisburg: Trinity Press, 1972), 106.

7. Notice God was forced to use a mediator to speak to them because that was what they demanded the last time he talked directly to them in Exodus 20:19.

Chapter 6 Actively Listening

1. See, for example, G. B. Armstrong and L. Chung, "Background television and reading memory in context," *Communication Research*, 27 (2000): 327–52; A. Furnham and L. Strabac, "Music is as distracting as noise: The differential distraction of background music and noise on the cognitive test performance of introverts and extraverts," *Ergonomics*, 45 (2002): 203–17; G. Armstrong and B. Greenburg, "Background television as an inhibitor of cognitive processing," *Human Communication Research*, 16 (1990): 355–86.

2. Eyal Ophir, Clifford Nass, and Anthony D. Wagner, "Cognitive Control in Media Multitaskers," *Proceedings of the National Academy of Sciences USA*, 106:15583–87.

3. Personal email correspondence, March 2011.

4. From the Muratorian Fragment, quoted in Bruce Metzger, *The Canon of the New Testament*, (Oxford: Oxford University Press, 1987), 195.

5. Ben Campbell Johnson, *The God Who Speaks: Learning the Language of God* (Grand Rapids: Eerdmans, 2004), 113.

6. I have explained in *The Gift of Church*, chapter 2, how God is uniquely present in the midst of the gathered worship assembly.

7. Stanley Hauerwas, *Hannah's Child* (Grand Rapids: Eerdmans, 2010), 176.

8. George Müller, *The Lord's Dealings with George Müller* (London: J. Nisbet, 1865) as cited by Andrew Murray, "With Christ in the School of Prayer," *The Deeper Christian Life and Other Writings* (Nashville: Thomas Nelson, 2000), 241–44.

Chapter 7 Lessons Learned

1. Priscilla Shirer, *Discerning the Voice of God: How to Recognize When God Speaks* (Chicago: Moody, 2007), 41, 86. The first quote is Carson's, the second is Farrar's.

2. Murray, *Deeper Christian Life and Other Writings*, 245.

3. Another example of this from the Bible is Jeremiah 43:1–3, where the people assume it is Baruch who is telling Jeremiah what to do rather than the Lord.

4. My supervisor, who was an excellent supervisor, ended up actually liking my topic by the end. God's faithfulness was incredible, but there were still great struggles along the way.

5. Lewis Sperry Chafer, *He That Is Spiritual* (Grand Rapids: Zondervan, 1918), 93.

Chapter 8 Telling Others

1. Hannah Whitall Smith, *The Christian's Secret of a Holy Life: The Unpublished Personal Writings of Hannah Whitall Smith*, Melvin E. Dieter, ed. (Oak Harbor: Logos, 1997).

2. Ben Campbell Johnson, *GodSpeech: Putting Divine Disclosures into Human Words* (Grand Rapids: Eerdmans, 2006), 75.

3. P. L. Tan, *Encyclopedia of 7700 Illustrations: Signs of the Times* (Garland, TX: Bible Communications, Inc., 1996), accessed through Logos Bible Software. Emphasis mine.

Chapter 9 Conclusion

1. Lewis Carroll, *Alice in Wonderland* (New York: MacMillan, 1897), 89–90. The text reads: " 'Would you tell me, please, which way I ought to walk from here?' 'That depends a good deal on where you want to get to,' said the Cat. 'I don't care much where—' said Alice. 'Then it doesn't matter which way you walk,' said the Cat. '—so long as I get somewhere,' Alice added as an explanation. 'Oh, you are sure to do that,' said the Cat, 'if only you walk long enough.' "

2. Even the designation *Father* seems to have grown out of ways of looking at and addressing God with regard to his wisdom, care, and guidance of our lives. Ben Witherington, *Jesus the Sage* (Minneapolis: Fortress Press, 1994), 386.

3. Charles Spurgeon, "Inquiring of God," *Sermons on the Will of God*, ed. Warren Wiersbe (Grand Rapids: Kregel, 1998), 146–48.

Appendix Frequently Asked Questions

1. Peter O'Brien comments on Ephesians 5:17, "In our contemporary context, the 'Lord's will' is frequently understood by Christians to refer to matters of personal guidance, and thus to God's immediate plans for their future. But the divine will in the Pauline letters, particularly in Ephesians, *has a different focus, without neglecting the personal dimension*" (emphasis mine). Peter O'Brien, *Ephesians* (Grand Rapids: Eerdmans, 1999), 386.

2. Haddon Robinson, *Decision Making by the Book* (Grand Rapids: Discovery House, 1998), 61.

3. Francis Watson observes that this is part of the nature of the Old Testament's religious legislation. It is embedded in narrative contexts. Francis Watson, *Text, Church and World* (Edinburgh: Continuum, 1994), 275.

4. Daniel Dorian makes a similar point in "A Redemptive-Historical Model," *Moving Beyond the Bible to Theology*, ed. Gary Meadors (Grand Rapids: Zondervan, 2009), 89. "Where a series of acts by the faithful create a pattern, and God or the narrator approves the pattern, it directs believers, even if no law spells out the lesson." See also John Goldingay's observation that scriptural narratives show us who God is and what it means to be human in "Biblical Narrative and Systematic Theology," *Between Two Horizons: Spanning New Testament Studies and Systematic Theology*, ed. Joel Green and Max Turner (Grand Rapids: Eerdmans, 2000), 123–42. Taken together the vast array of guidance narratives in the Bible show us first and foremost that God is a loving God who guides his people through the pathways of life. The narratives also show that we as humans need such guidance and direction.

5. Gordon Wenham, *Story as Torah* (Edinburgh: T&T Clark, 2000).

6. This translation is adapted from John Goldingay, *Psalms* vol. 1 (Grand Rapids: Baker, 2006), 350. He reminds us that 23:3 is not "introducing a moral note and asking to be led to live the right kind of life. Faithful paths are paths consistent with the divine shepherd's faithfulness."

Jim Samra is probably a little crazy, but God has chosen him to be a servant of Jesus Christ and to minister as the senior pastor of Calvary Church in Grand Rapids, Michigan, a job that forces him to depend on God daily. Jim has a PhD from Oxford University, a ThM from Dallas Theological Seminary, and a BS from the University of Michigan. He is also the author of *The Gift of Church* and *Being Conformed to Christ in Community*. Jim and his wife Lisa have four amazing children, and therefore spend a lot of time listening for guidance from God.

Keep LISTENING.
Keep GROWING.

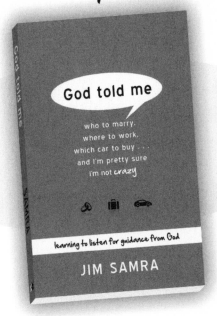

Visit **www.GodToldMetheBook.com** for resources and help listening to God.

Equip and engage your small group or entire church too!

- Video message from Jim Samra
- Group discussion starters, tips, and downloads
- Free sermon outlines
- Promotional resources
- Additional "God Told Me" stories